General editor: Graham Handley MA PhD

Brodie's Notes on Joseph Heller's

Catch-22

Graham Handley MA PhD
Formerly Principal Lecturer in English, College of All Saints, Tottenham

Pan Books London and Sydney

Extracts from Joseph Heller's *Catch-22* are reprinted by kind permission of Jonathan Cape Ltd.

This revised edition published 1987 by Pan Books Ltd,
Cavaye Place, London SW10 9PG
9 8 7 6 5 4 3 2 1
© Graham Handley 1987
ISBN 0 330 50253 0
Photoset by Parker Typesetting Service, Leicester
Printed and bound in Great Britain by
Richard Clay (The Chaucer Press) Ltd, Bungay, Suffolk

Contents

Page references in these notes are to the
Corgi edition of *Catch-22*, but references are
also given to particular chapters, so that the
notes may be used with any edition of the book

Preface

The intention throughout this study aid is to stimulate and guide, to encourage the reader's *involvement* in the text, to develop disciplined critical responses and a sure understanding of the main details.

Brodie's Notes provide a summary of the plot of the play or novel followed by act, scene or chapter summaries, each of which will have an accompanying critical commentary designed to emphasize the most important literary and factual details. Poems, stories or non-fiction texts will combine brief summary with critical commentary on either individual aspects or sequences of the genre being considered. Textual notes will be explanatory or critical (sometimes both), defining what is difficult or obscure on the one hand, or stressing points of character, style, plot or the technical aspects of poetry on the other. Revision questions will be set at appropriate points to test the student's careful application to the text of the prescribed book.

The second section of each of these study aids will consist of a critical examination of the author's art. This will cover such major elements as characterization, style, structure, setting, theme(s) for example in novels, plays or stories; in poetry it will deal with the types of poem, rhyme, rhythm, free verse for example, or in non-fiction with the main literary concerns of the work. The editor may choose to examine any aspect of the book being studied which he or she considers to be important. The paramount aim is to send the student back to the text. Each study aid will include a series of general questions which require detailed knowledge of the set book: the first of these questions will have notes by the editor of what *might* be included in a written answer. A short list of books considered useful as background reading for the student will be provided at the end.

The General Certificate of Secondary Education in Literature

These study aids are suitable for candidates taking the new GCSE examinations in English Literature since they provide detailed preparation for examinations in that subject as well as presenting critical ideas and commentary of major use to candidates preparing their coursework files. These aids provide a basic, individual and imaginative response to the appreciation of literature. They stimulate disciplined habits of reading, and they will assist the responsive student to analyse and to write about the texts with discrimination and insight.

Graham Handley

The author and his work

There has always been a certain elusiveness about the life and work of Joseph Heller, though the one-novel man of 1961 has certainly proved to be far from that. Interviews with him over the years have been sparse, and contemporary biographical dictionaries and literary yearbooks generally accord him little or no space. There are now quite a few essays and critical articles and some chapters and references in books dealing with the contemporary novel to Heller, more particularly since he has contributed three other novels of considerable literary status and best-seller impact.

Has *Catch-22*, having sired *M*A*S*H* among others, lost its appeal for today's readers? I think not. *Catch-22* is in the great tradition of English satire, the tradition of Swift in *Gulliver's Travels*, of Samuel Butler in *Erewhon*, and of George Orwell in *Animal Farm*. Its degraded generals are, as John Wain has correctly said, a Dickensian crew. The area of attack in the novel is limited by time and location, yet in a sense it is for all time and all locations which have to do with war – which tolerate it, make it, exploit it. The reverberations of that attack confront the Western world with the manifestations of its own sickness, as terribly relevant today as they were in the sixties – or the forties – or the teens of this century. The verbal acid of *Catch-22* has burned a hole that cannot easily be welded over. Since the early 1960s satire – in print, theatre, films and television – has castigated the vices and follies of the times. These exposures have brought legal and political clashes with the establishment, witness, in this country, cases against the magazine *Private Eye*.

In Heller's case, in *Catch-22*, the message was anything but ephemeral. John Wain tells us that the book was eight years in the writing and, prior to that, eight years in gestation. The next novel, *Something Happened* (1971), shows Heller's capacity to translate to a peace-time role without any loss of direction or any muting of his language. This time the major concern is the executive establishment, with the narrative in the first person and encompassing, as always in Heller, that clever mix of the past and the present. There are many laughs, but it is, like

Catch-22, a sad book once you start to think about the impact, the deep layers of consciousness, sexuality, fear and degradation which are uncovered. The running battle of domesticity with wife and children, the power struggle which negates integrity in the office, the sordid ease of drink and casual sex, in other words, the American way of life which is seen as death, all this is Heller's world. Like *Catch-22*, it is a brave book. Seldom has the lust of the past been made so meaningfully, frighteningly present in the degradation of middle age.

Good as Gold was issued in book form in 1979, and in his own middle age (he was born in 1923) Heller proves to have lost none of his sharpness. Basically he covers three areas in this memorable comedy, sick and black as ever, in tracing the mythical career of Bruce Gold, dishonest Professor of Literature, writer and family man caught up in the family prison of relations. The send-up of Jewish family life is superbly sustained, but more of this later. The second area has Gold searching for the Jewish experience, committed to writing about it but keeping a scrapbook about Henry Kissinger so that he can produce a book on him. The third – and they are all interrelated – has Gold as a presidential aide – he never, of course, sees the president – his part that of cliché phrasemaker whose words pass for wisdom because they are the direct opposite of it.

The Jewish family scenes are hilarious, with Gold as victim of his own success in his father's eyes. That father is one of the funniest characters in contemporary fiction, bullying, grotesque, irascible, complacent, gifted, at a time when many are senile, with demented energy. Running him close for pride of place is the millionaire Pugh Biddle Conover, who becomes a second father to Gold in terms of insults but not in fact, since Gold never leaves his wife Esther to marry the tall, willowy Andrea, Conover's daughter of limitless but usually failed sexual experience. But perhaps the most important area of this brilliant book is the satire on the government, or perhaps one should say more correctly non-government, with its camouflage of spokesmen, sources, archaisms in terms of people, corruption, the whole gamut of non-administration. One is tempted to say that Henry Kissinger lives by virtue of Gold's maliciously selected clips.

After war, executive life and government, what more natural than that Heller should turn to God, the Bible and, specifically, David, of David and Goliath fame. Old Testament time is subsumed in all succeeding time in order to give David the freedom to tell his own story against the unfolding panorama of later events. The area explored is as sexual and corrupt as ever, the humour as sudden and cataclysmic as any biblical event. *God Knows* is a major novel in the Heller tradition. I'm not sure that it is quite as funny as *Good as Gold*, but it is certainly as irreverent (and in this case that is the right word). And let me add that the Jewish experience is very much a part of this novel.

It is impossible in surveying the work of a great writer to do justice in a brief introduction to the nature of his claims to greatness. Heller's voice is brave, relentless, unswerving, producing the fireworks of the unexpected, the sick or subtle wit (often about the terrible reality), and the scintillating send-up. His insistent reiterations are like the insistent reiterations of life – or dreams – or art. He modulates between the first-person narrator or a central character who recognizably has his sympathies, the Yossarian of the war or the Gold of a stigmatized peacetime existence. His is a sustained technique, brilliantly informed with imagination, pursuing truths that no longer exist in our world. Perhaps his highest art is the art of compulsion. Take the opening of *Catch-22*; 'It was love at first sight. The first time Yossarian saw the chaplain he fell in love with him.' Is it a trick, a gimmick, gay, sick? Whatever our reaction, we have to go on reading, for we have been 'conned' by the immediate impact of the unusual. In a way, but it is a way into other ways of the heart and the mind, this is the most effective device in *Catch-22*, and discerning critics have been quick to accord Heller the serious attention denied to the literary con-man.

Catch-22 is an unusual novel, and a long and, in this writer's opinion, a carefully-structured one. Adopt a disciplined and imaginative approach, looking at the techniques as you read, noting the main concerns, the objects of satire, the terrors of reality, and then look at this study aid and see if you agree with the main guidelines towards appreciation of this novel. War turns the world upside down for those who are in it, and Heller shows with searing insight what it does to man and what man does to himself as a result.

Background and setting

Although the setting is described as 'fictitious' and, in the circumstances, there would be little point in any exact location (though Pianosa does exist and it *is* eight miles south of Elba), there is little doubt that an interested student, examining the text closely (when did Rome and Bologna fall? when did the Germans launch a counter-attack at Antwerp?) could identify much of the factual background to the novel. Pianosa may be merely the cover name for a US Air base, but it is quite clear that we are in 1944 and within striking distance of the Italian mainland. D-day (6 June 1944) had seen the invasion of German-occupied Europe via France and the Low Countries; in the early months of 1944 there was but slow progress on the Italian front. The overall commitment of the US Air Force on the Italian front was to provide close air support for Allied troops, though there was thought to be some friction between the Americans and the British. There was the task of continually attacking the German supply lines in Italy; and the overall idea was to eliminate the German forces in Italy and begin an operation (*Anvil*) the object of which was to open up ports in Southern France, so that the forty or fifty divisions waiting in the United States could land and strike up to join Eisenhower's troops advancing from the other side. The French captured Elba on 19 June 1944, so it seems that the action of *Catch-22* – or part of it, in view of the time switches – comes after that date. And the constant references to the Pacific – and the graves in the Solomon Islands – lend support to this view. Because of bad weather, 'Anvil' did not begin until 15 August 1944, when the British Eighth Army began its advance through the Apennines, and the American Seventh Army landed on the Riviera beaches and advanced rapidly up the Rhone valley, joining hands with Eisenhower's troops at Dijon (fifty thousand German soldiers being captured). Since Yossarian's squadron was involved in attacks on Avignon and Bologna, it seems likely that the reason for the number of missions being constantly raised by the execrable Cathcart was because they were supporting both the advance through Italy and the attack on Southern France.

Chapter commentaries, textual notes and revision questions

You will find that the early chapters are noted more fully than the later ones: this is to establish in your mind the setting, the characters, the techniques and the areas of satire. Thus the details must be absorbed by the student as he reads this study aid, so that by the time he reaches the later chapters the habit of critical reading and noting will enable him to fill in many of the stylistic and satirical effects for himself.

Chapter 1, The Texan

Yossarian in hospital with supposed liver pains, his temperature as always 101, indiscriminately censoring letters. He pretends in letters to his friends that he is on a dangerous mission; the other members of the ward described, the Texan of the chapter title being the odd man out because he is actually conventional and patriotic. He has no understanding of the 'sick' joke that he has killed the patient who dies, and who was encased in plaster. Yossarian has a cliché-conversation with the chaplain, there is a description of the mess-hall fire, and a short account of the Colonel 'in the small private section at the end of the ward'. The goodness of the Texan clears the ward, for nobody can stand him.

Note that Yossarian is intent on getting out of the combat situation by his act, and that there is considerable wit involved in the censoring of the letters. This, like the war itself, takes no account of the emotional injuries done to people. The fire incident seems to indicate inefficiency, while the essential naiveté and goodness of the chaplain are stressed. The Colonel and his visitor are given the sentimental, romantic treatment, rather as if we are being invited to look at a representation on film. This is a typical Heller technique. There is little doubt that the Texan is being sent-up for his views, which imply a hidebound insensitivity.

It was love at first sight Notice the unexpectedness of the opening, and its ridiculous statement, which isn't true. As we get into the novel, we shall learn that part of the *humour* is the making of arresting statements which have no substance.

jaundice Notice that the word is mentioned five times in the second paragraph – another typical Heller stylistic device, that of deliberate *repetition.*

to censor letters This was required in wartime, in case letters home containing information were intercepted by the enemy.

enlisted-men patients Much play is made in the novel of army snobbery between the officers on the one hand and the ordinary 'conscripts' on the other.

articles i.e. 'the' and 'a'.

a much higher plane of creativity Note the *irony* of the phrase in view of what he is doing.

dynamic intralinear tensions This time the irony is Yossarian's own; intra meaning 'within' – he is generating excitement by what he deletes.

obliterating whole homes and streets Yossarian is doing this metaphorically, but the phrase carries overtones of the destruction caused by bombing in wartime.

Washington Irving It's a good choice, being the name of the popular American essayist and historian (1783–1859).

ethereal military echelon Again the ironic tone is apparent from the choice of high-flown language.

C.I.D. Criminal Investigation Department. The censorship section here is part of Heller's satire against what is largely unnecessary and what is irresponsibly done as service routine.

Adriatic Sea i.e. between the Italian mainland and Yugoslavia.

grippe Influenza.

they were so interesting they were foolish Heller's use of *paradox* runs throughout the novel – Yossarian as rebel is established by his doing the opposite of what the normal, conventional person would do.

people of means . . . people without means This is a satirical attack upon the Texan who believes, to paraphrase George Orwell's words in *Animal Farm*, that some people are more equal than others.

unspringing rhythms Sprung rhythm, used by the poet Gerard Manley Hopkins, is dependent on stress; so presumably Yossarian is taking out the 'stress' he finds in the letters.

cultivating boredom This is Dunbar's salient characteristic.

'There was something missing' Dunbar is being heavily sarcastic, implying that they have had too much 'patriotism'.

the Brooklyn Dodgers . . . Mom's apple pie Both symbolize love of what has been left behind at home: the famous baseball team, and home cooking – two of the sentimental 'calls to duty' a 'this-is-what-we-are-fighting-to-preserve-theme' common in wartime and despised (now they have seen the reality of war) by people like Yossarian and Dunbar.

matriotism Part of the wit of *Catch-22* is to be found in the swiftness of the repartee. Here Yossarian coins his own word with its associations of America as a mother – though it may even look beyond to a kind of matriarchal society.

The soldier in white The whole of this paragraph should be read with close attention. The satire on medical inefficiency is beginning, but this patient symbolizes death, the anonymous deaths of all those who die or who suffer the terrible wounds which leave them to a living death.

The Texan never minded that he got no reply Heller's shafts are many and barbed, for this suggests the kind of egoism and insensitivity that doesn't listen anyway. The Texan's limitations are further exposed – his decency is only skin-deep – when he says 'They got a special place for niggers.'

'You murdered him ... I heard you kill him' A fine early example of the 'send-up' technique employed by Yossarian and Dunbar here and generally directed against those who represent the establishment – the respectable. Notice the crispness, tongue-in-cheek quality of the dialogue: almost like a comic cross-talk act.

a stove exploded Again, this paragraph is satirical of army inefficiency, which has the firemen moving from a fire to something that hasn't even happened – and then having to return again.

romance words i.e. from the Romance languages (Italian, French etc).

'That's good ... that is too bad' This is a wonderful satirical rendering of cliché conversation, non-communication which passes for contact and understanding. Heller has a fine ear for this kind of nothingness.

all that's humanly possible Irony, for the phrase has become a meaningless cliché.

Yossarian was sorry to hear they had a mutual friend Paradox again, typical of Yossarian's attitude, which is always anti-conventional on principle.

a bad start ... a good family Another paradox, reversing usually held beliefs.

That's two to the fighting eighth power ... writing a symbolic poem Yossarian is being very ironic, playing with arithmetic and literature, mocking the statisticians and the patriotic poets at one and the same time.

chaplain Notice how often the word is used – another example of repetition and cliché conversation.

An innocent nest of ancient pimple pricks What begins as a conventional image turns out to be a realistic one – unromantic, unsentimental.

Father Yossarian is being ironic again, giving the chaplain a false position in another faith.

M.P.s Military police. This looks forward to Yossarian's later arrest.

least dedicated men A paradox again, but Yossarian means it!

three votes In view of the Texan's known views, Yossarian is sending him up.

Wac Women's Auxiliary Corps.

Communications Signals, codes. The 'sick' joke is followed through in the rest of the paragraph where the Colonel transmits 'glutinous messages', i.e. mucus, phlegm, vomit.

urologist ... cetologist A fine satire on specialism in medicine-over-specialization in fact – together with the disproportionate numbers of specialists allocated to one man.

shanghaied i.e. forced.

I.B.M. machine A punch-card record of a man's aptitudes is referred to here.

Moby Dick The classic novel about a whale, by Herman Melville (1819–91).

drugged and derogated Notice the alliterative effects which make for a parody of pompous tone.

broke i.e. down, gave in.

and come down with pneumonia The implication is, in an ironic aside at the end of the chapter, that this is poetic justice.

Chapter 2, Clevinger

Flashback to Clevinger, and his assuring Yossarian that no one is trying to kill him; this is Yossarian's obsession – a reasonable one, we may think, for someone in wartime. Yossarian lives with Orr in a tent on the island of Pianosa. McWatt shares one with Clevinger, who has not returned when Yossarian comes out of hospital. Yossarian recalls the night at the officers' club when his argument with the rational Clevinger had occurred. Colonel Cathcart is continually increasing the number of combat missions everyone has to fly. The name 'Clevinger' at the head of the chapter is another aspect of Heller's irony – perhaps a send-up of traditional novels – for only a small part of the chapter actually deals with Clevinger.

Clevinger's reasoning with Yossarian provides the classic definition of the madness of war and at the same time defines Yossarian's obsession with being killed himself. There is some fine description (note the physical account of Orr) and some anticipation of McWatt's fatal action later. The tensions are increased in this chapter, for the reader may well ask if there is any sanity in it. The answer would appear to be that war produces various levels of individual insanity or reflex opportunism, from crazy orders to the award of medals to men who lost their minds.

Men went mad and were rewarded with medals This is the first overt anti-war statement, equating war with insanity in its effects.

infundibuliform Funnel-shaped, but Heller is fond of using the long and unusual word at times, and this one is probably intended as a parody of pedantic utterance.

He was really very sick Another paradox – being normal is a form of sickness in Yossarian's mind – and perhaps in Heller's too.

He was crazy The implication is that to have 'principles' is mad.

a placid blue sea . . . that could gulp down a person The somewhat poetic personification hides the terrible reality that death is near.

a breeze that never blew The satire is here directed against the fact that we are ruled by habit.

the dead man in Yossarian's tent He is a statistic (we later find out what happened) and the satire is against the military concern with 'numbers' rather than with people.

flew his plane as low as he dared This idea of McWatt's capacity for danger prepares us for what happens later to Kid Sampson.

Yossarian had not helped build Again a reversal of the normal – we are proud of what we do, not of what we didn't do.

God, Motherhood and The American Way of Life The capital letters underline the fact that these standbys of sentimental appeal are under attack.

Ferrara . . . Bologna Italian cities of the North, of strategic importance.

Assyrian Possibly this makes him more of an outsider, though in view of the mixed nationalities which make up America (and the mixture of names in the novel) it does not appear to be significant.

Tarzan, Mandrake, Flash Gordon The first the legendary Jungle strong man created by Edgar Rice Burroughs, the second a comic-strip magician, the third a comic-strip superman.

Cain Brother of Abel, whom he had put to death.

Ulysses i.e. the Greek Odysseus, one of the heroes of the Trojan war, the subject of Homer's epic *The Odyssey*.

the Flying Dutchman The Dutch captain fated for his sins to scour the sea and never reach port, and the title of an opera by Wagner on the subject.

Lot in Sodom See Genesis 13, 5–13. He was delivered from the destruction of the cities of the plain, and was the father of Moab and Ammon.

Deidre of the Sorrows, Sweeney in the nightingales among trees Two literary references, the first to the uncompleted tragedy by the Irish playwright J. M. Synge (1871–1909), the second to a poem by T. S. Eliot (1888–1965) called *Sweeney Among the Nightingales*.

supraman Yossarian is playing on the word, which means 'above' – he may be thinking of himself as a bomb aimer (above the target) or even sexually (on top of).

Jehovah The name by which God revealed himself to the Hebrews.

Nathaniel One of Christ's disciples, commended by Jesus for his guilelessness.

Raskolnikov Leading character in Dostoievsky's *Crime and Punishment*.
a sensible young gentleman The language is mocking, the very
 opposite of the real Yossarian.
in Smyrna for the fig harvest The first indication we have of the
 buying and selling activities of Milo. Smyrna, now known as Izmir, is in
 Turkey.
like a broken suspender Occasionally Heller employs the simple,
 domestic image.
marinating Soaking in wine or vinegar mixed with olive oil.
the Levant Syria, Lebanon, Israel.
Benedictine A liqueur.
de Coverley An ironically-chosen name, since Sir Roger de Coverley, a
 character in Addison's and Steele's *The Spectator*, is the benevolent type
 of English squire of the reign of Queen Anne (1702–1714). Sir Roger
 de Coverley is also the name of a dance.
fifty missions i.e. fifty bombing raids. Much of the novel hinges on the
 unscrupulous way in which the number of missions is always being
 raised.
spatulate (face) The racket-shaped end of a bird's tail-feather, again
 indicative of Heller's tendency to employ the unusual word on
 occasions.

Chapter 3, Havermeyer

Orr fiddling with the gas stove, and going into his long and
seemingly pointless story about the crab apples in his cheeks –
part of the humour lies in the pointlessness of what is recounted
from time to time, just as in life. One of the recurring motifs of
the novel underlines this – the story of Orr in Rome being hit
over the head with a shoe until he is knocked cold by the girl.
The account switches to the feuding at top brass level – that
between Generals Peckem and Dreedle. Wintergreen's role –
and power – in the feud is described, and this is followed by the
appeal/order of the successfully unsuccessful Colonel Cargill to
the men to attend the U.S.O. performance. Havermeyer, un-
popular because he is a daring bombardier, shoots field-mice at
night and Hungry Joe, in the middle of a nightmare, fires into
Havermeyer's tent.

All this is a searching and uncompromising examination of
the neurosis of war, which brings out psychological obsessions,
as we see in the case of Orr, Havermeyer and Hungry Joe. The
visual effects are particularly strong in this chapter. The satire
against the feuding top brass, the power complex which deter-
mines motives, the frightful level of casual non-communication

and irresponsible and petty action, all these are part of Heller's exposure here.

the dead man i.e. who exists in the records, not in reality.

anything ... anything ... crab-apples One of Orr's characteristics is that he is able to match Yossarian for words.

with the tip of his tongue in one of his apple cheeks i.e. Yossarian feels that Orr is mocking him.

beating him over the head with her shoe This whole sequence, which is repeated from time to time, underlines another facet of Heller's style – his concern with the visual and the grotesque. Part of the technique of the novel is the re-iteration of incidents which are repeated in the consciousness, or memory, so that there is a unity between the inward and the outward in experience.

shim-sham-shimmying The effect is of a tremulous, vibrating, strongly rhythmic dance.

bonanza the word means 'pay off' or 'prosperity' and is being used ironically here.

for the daily amusement of the dying, ignorant armies clashed by night ... Heller is at one and the same moment attacking the Hollywood war films ('ignorant' because they do not express the reality of war experience) and at one remove echoing piognantly Matthew Arnold's *Dover Beach:* 'And we are here as on a darkling plain/Swept with confused alarms of struggle and flight,/Where ignorant armies clash by night.' These lines have an obvious application to the war situation Heller is describing.

U.S.O. United Services Organization, providing welfare, recreation, entertainment for the Armed Forces.

Peckem ... Dreedle The names alone are Dickensian.

enhanced ... increased Irony directed at the user of the high-flown 'literary' words.

prick Obscene sexual reference, indicative of contempt.

entrances facing back proudly toward the Washington Monument A fine satiric thrust at the meaningless nature of so many army orders and decisions.

these overlords Note the irony.

ex-P.F.C. Wintergreen Important character because he takes far-reaching decisions – ironic, since he is an 'ex Private First Class', and has been demoted – further satire at the expense of military organization.

like useless young men in a depression Notice that Heller's range goes beyond the present; the unemployment of the thirties – another area of human suffering – is in the forefront of his mind here.

troubleshooter Man who detects and corrects faults.

firms eager to establish losses for tax purposes Superb satirical sequence attacking big business and its devious practices.

Battery Park to Fulton Street The first a small park on the Hudson

River side of Manhattan. The second is on the East River side, and has a fish market.

a self-made man who owed his lack of success to nobody i.e. he is responsible for his own inability – again the ironic reversal of a cliché.

But that girl . . . is old enough to be a mother Colonel Cargill's address to the men plays on all the sentimental appeal, the false emotion, the drummed-up response. Here it is a fine parody of the manner. Ironically, it ends with an order!

peanuts . . . chicken feed i.e. small amounts. Note the continuing use of cliché in these exchanges – an echo of real life.

do just about nothing A reverse, as we have come to expect, of the normal.

dumdummed i.e. so that they would 'split' and cause more suffering, evidence of Havermeyer's sadistic streak.

the I.P. Initial point. The beginning of a bombing run.

flung out all over the sky like prayers In view of what 'flak' does, this is a casually ironic image. ('Flak' is anti-aircraft fire.)

Sturm und Drang German for 'storm and stress'.

Captain Aardvaark This is a joke name, for the aardvark (spelt with a slight difference) is a South African quadruped, something between an armadillo and an ant-eater.

Havermeyer would chortle exultantly . . . its timid soul back to his or her creator This is symbolic of what has happened to man and how, perhaps because of wartime pressures, he takes a sadistic delight in killing for killing's sake. The ingenuity of Havermeyer's 'trap' mirrors on a small scale the ingenuity of man in making weapons that torture and destroy man.

Milo Minderbinder had bombed the squadron Part of Heller's technique is to switch backwards and forwards in time. This incident is recounted, together with the motive behind it, with sickening satire later in the novel.

when tongueless dead men peopled the night hours like living ghosts Heller can reproduce the macabre, nightmare effect, and does so here not as an extension of Hungry Joe's dreams but as the reality of men who were killed – who can therefore no longer speak.

Chapter 4, Doc Daneeka

The latter broods over his health, and over 'the Pacific Ocean and flight time'. There is an account of the 'educational sessions' disrupted by Yossarian, and the death of Snowden (later to be expanded upon with realistic detail). The feuding generals are further confused by the non-code name 'T. S. Eliot', and there is some emphasis on the organized skeet-shooting. The satire is largely directed, in this chapter, against aspects of military time-wasting, ignorance, bad organization and bureaucracy.

There is a considered satire too against, for example, the taking of temperatures, and a detailed exposure of the neurosis of Doc Daneeka. The sick humour about Snowden shows the deep fears and obsessions of Yossarian himself. Again the pettiness of the top brass quarrel is emphasized, but the whole code-area is ridiculed in the T. S. Eliot joke, which at the same time reveals wholesale cultural ignorance.

shooting their kissers off i.e. talking too loudly, 'shooting their mouths off'.

to have his temperature taken Doc Daneeka's salient characteristic is his hypochondria, and much of the satire directed at medical inefficiency in this early section is focused on him.

gums and toes painted . . . a laxative to throw away Further satire on the tendency to prescribe what is useless rather than trying to find out what is wrong.

pitching horseshoes Ironic appraisal of the tendency to play 'games' to pass the time before the big 'game' of war makes demands on you.

motor pool i.e. those held in readiness with vehicles, transport.

a subconscious desire to climb back into the womb Later there is a much more extended attack on psychiatry, but this is the first manifestation of it – a satirical glance at the American dependence on analysis, the talking-out of complexes and obsessions.

persuade McWatt to enter Doc Daneeka's name on his flight log Fundamental dishonesty, 'fiddling', is one of the basic ingredients of army life, and Heller does not omit mention of small manifestations of it.

grease i.e. bribes.

Yossarian began scratching his back Another aspect of the humour is the literal response, for Doc Daneeka was of course talking metaphorically on the 'I'll help you, you help me' level.

who never stopped feeling sorry for himself i.e. irony, for all his 'warmth' is given to himself.

subversive i.e. undermining the establishment.

Adolf Hitler Heller is being ironic about Black's view, for Hitler virtually destroyed Communism in Europe; and at the time of *Catch-22* and earlier, many Americans who had been members of the Communist Party were accused of 'un-American activities'.

'Who is Spain?' This whole sequence is fine comedy, for the questions are deliberate nonsense. The reference to Spain would reflect the anti-Franco feeling of the Americans. (Franco's forces won the Spanish Civil War in the late thirties and he then set up a Fascist dictatorship which was, while they remained officially 'neutral', supported by Hitler and by Mussolini the Italian leader.)

the merry-go-round broke down This is a line from a popular song of the time.

'beriberi' Disease of malnutrition in the East. This reference perhaps reflects the fears that the men might be sent east to fight the Japanese.

'balls' Merely indicates contempt for the 'educational sessions'. The asking of the unanswerable looks forward to the questions in Chapter 39, The Eternal City – the suffering that cannot be answered.

'Where are the Snowdens of yesteryear? ... *Oú sont les Neigedens d'antan?'* There is the constant reminder of the death of Snowden, and this passing mention looks forward to the full realistic treatment later in the novel. The famous quotation half punned by Yossarian ('Where are the snows of yesteryear?') is from the *'Ballade des Dames du Temps Jadis'*, by the French poet François Villon (1431–85).

'*Je ne parle pas français.'* The joke is that by saying this the corporal is demonstrating that he does speak French!

there was no telling what people might find out Ironic appraisal of army reaction, which leads of course to repression of all questions.

with the exception of the chaplain An ironic underlining of the fact that the *spiritual* element is placed deliberately outside main army concerns.

skeet Clay targets simulating birds in flight.

homiletic i.e. sermonizing.

one poet who makes money ... T. S. Eliot This is the humour of slick movement in the narrative, for we switch from Cargill to Wintergreen uttering the name, cryptically, on the phone. There is an adhesive of truth – T. S. Eliot (see note p.15) wrote criticism, drama, poetry, and was the director of a publishing firm – he certainly made money. The mention of his name reflects the lack of culture (they don't know who he is) among the top brass.

It trained them to shoot skeet An ironic comment on what it didn't do – it didn't improve them in any way!

Chapter 5, Chief White Halfoat

The Chief is Doc Daneeka's tent companion. The Doc tells the story of the virgin bride: the humour lies in the fact that we don't know why he was punched on the nose – perhaps because he made the man lose face in front of his wife. The next area of humour is that explored by the Chief, who gives a (lying) account of always being moved on as the white men drilled for oil wherever they found Indians. Yossarian, intent on being grounded, finds himself up against the classic definition of *Catch-22* (p.54); there is the joke about Appleby having flies in his eyes; and yet another reference to the mission to Avignon when Dobbs went crazy in mid-air and Snowden was dying. This is the nightmare core of the novel, constantly present in Yossarian's consciousness: the terrible reality of war.

The satire here is directed at dishonest medical practice (the Doc tries to get himself classified as unfit) and at the fact that anyone is accepted into the services and often allocated to unsuitable tasks. The underlying theme too embraces the fact that men are cowards, not brave, as propaganda would have everyone believe. The linking of sanity and madness (war=madness) is encapsulated in Doc Daneeka's definition of *Catch-22*. Briefly, there is no escape from the war situation.

Staten Island New York. It is a large sand-bar with docks.

firetrap i.e. fraught with danger in terms of being easily set fire to.

his adding machine was repossessed Satire here against a way of life which depends on hire purchase.

upped my kickback fee i.e. paid more to be protected. The satire here is directed against corruption in the medical profession, as personified by Doc Daneeka, who even examines himself and gives himself an 'unfit to serve' grade.

'It's a terrible thing' Doc is nothing if not a hypocrite!

Saint Anthony The patron saint of swineherds – ironically used here, but the repetition of the name is part of the 'dumb' conversation carried on by Doc and the young couple.

compact kit of injustices Economic metaphor, with army kit in mind, to describe Doc's misery.

pimp of a snotnose Derogatory comment on Wintergreen; but note the fact that current slang and innuendo is employed, as we should expect – though not necessarily from an Indian.

Oklahoma Large state; and the town of Enid, the Chief's town, is located there.

loused it up with their goddam piety Perhaps a reference to the missionary quality of the white settlers.

barely read or write . . . assistant intelligence officer Another caustic comment on the way the army mishandles people, though the Chief's use of language – 'human divining rods . . . natural affinity' – indicates that he has a flair for idiom: yet another paradox.

Petroleum deposits i.e. oil.

the stock market turned bullish i.e. there was an attempt to raise prices.

the jump i.e. to get in before.

wouldn't accept Indians as guests Indication of prejudice which, we see from the next statement, breeds intolerance and further prejudice.

kike, wop or spic Derogatory slang – Jews (of Slavonic origin), an Italian, a Mexican.

kick us off i.e. get rid of us.

draft board i.e. responsible for calling men up for the services in wartime.

I was the only survivor A satirical way of indicating peacetime pressures in the language of wartime.

because they were red i.e. not white, a sick joke.

Indian wrestle Two wrestlers, elbows on table: each tries to force down the other's hand on to the table.

There was only one catch This paragraph is the key to the novel: the trap, the who-is-crazy, who-is-sane question which is answered in simple terms – ask to be grounded and you are revealing that you are sane and therefore fit to fly!

elliptical precision about its perfect pairs of parts There is irony in this too, probably this high-flown language and what it describes (Catch-22) would be best summarized by the word 'balls' in Yossarian's mind.

flies in his eyes A flippant version of the Catch-22 joke.

wilderness outside New York City Irony again, since he is thinking in terms of overcrowding rather than freedom.

milk run to Parma On the main line between Bologna and Milan. A 'milk run' means a 'delivery' of bombs that encounters no opposition.

Sties flies Humour in the half-heard word 'sties' making better sense than 'flies'.

The three enlisted men in each crew were not briefed A further instance of military inefficiency, and hence satire against snobbery.

like sightless, stupid, crippled things A fine way of describing the movement of aircraft on the ground – they are not really alive until they enter their own element, the sky.

cerulean Rather poetic word meaning 'deep-blue'. It contrasts strongly with the remainder of the paragraph, which is rooted in the realism, the habitual ritual of the flight.

inside a sheltering igloo of extra flak suits The comparison is apt in terms of the appearance, and also in terms of the 'cold' – that is, the feeling of death – the cold constantly referred to by Snowden.

goldfish . . . goldfish bowl This conveys the unprotected nature of the bombardier and the gunners in their plexiglass turrets in the aircraft.

flak Anti-aircraft fire.

climbing, cracking, staggered Read on to get the full force of the single-word effects, which convey both the movement and the fear.

ravenous pillars Fine image to convey the 'hunger' of death.

a dedicated fraternity man i.e. full of brotherly love, and membership of the right societies – conventional and hence despised, as Yossarian reveals from time to time.

Hard, hard, hard Referring to moving the plane sharply in the direction he wants.

Help him, help him The pathetic words convey the anguish of Dobbs, the unhinging of the man under the terrible stress of the moment.

Chapter 6, Hungry Joe

At this stage in the narrative he has done fifty-three missions and has nightmares which wake everyone except his under-age tent-mate Huple. Hungry Joe is always in a hurry, always trying to persuade naked girls to pose, always taking pictures which never come out. The irony of his story is that he never quite flies enough missions to be sent home – nor of course does anyone else. Joe's nightmares cease when he returns to combat duty. The fight between Orr and Appleby is described; Flume's obsession that Chief White Halfoat is going to cut his (Flume's) throat when he is asleep; and the appointment of Major Major as 'new squadron commander'. Yossarian (at this stage having flown forty-eight missions) thinks that he can go home, but Doc Daneeka points out that 'Catch-22 . . . says you've always got to do what your commanding officer tells you to do.'

There is a terrible irony running throughout this chapter, which is a deepening of the Catch-22 situation in terms of the neuresthenic conditions in war. Hungry Joe's speed is frenetic, the reflex of a maddened man, but the irony referred to above is seen in the fact that his only peace of mind is obtained in flying combat missions. His punching Colonel Moodus on the nose is a moment of slapstick comedy. The actions and reactions often have a kind of crazy logic which is part of the technique of the novel.

fifty grand Fifty thousand. Doc's speech reflects his concern for money.
they had to manufacture fascism The implication that it is not *real* shows the complete selfishness of Doc's attitude.
motile i.e. capable of motion.
subcutaneously . . . like severed sections of snake Heller's language is richly figurative, and this simile vividly conveys the neurotic twitch.
like an abandoned mining town Another simile to indicate the desolation, the essential neurosis of Hungry Joe.
dinero i.e. money.
ficky-fick Sexual intercourse.
Women killed Hungry Joe i.e. equivalent to the phrase, 'you slay me': they fascinated him. The rest of the paragraph shows the nature of his obsession. He is always in a hurry, whether sexually or photographically.
furgle As for 'ficky-fick' above.
really had been a photographer Heller is adept at suddenly slipping in the most unlikely statement – but since much of *Catch-22* measures the success of failure, this is not surprising.

Salerno beachhead South along the coast from Naples. A beachhead was established there in September 1943.

burst of clap Venereal disease.

an eaten shell of a human building rocking perilously Note the appropriateness of this simile – buildings, like men, were smashed by the war.

like the mating calls of songbirds with filthy minds Irony: a deliberate reversal of the romantic associations of birdsong.

the nightmares stopped Again a reversal of what usually happens; here Hungry Joe is obsessed when he is *not* fighting. He has what Heller calls 'an inverted set of responses'.

the bombsight that could put bombs into a pickle barrel What is missing in military calculations is the most important element – the human one.

on the seventh day, while God was resting A superbly ironic and cynical appraisal of death – and the satirical attack on blind, conventional, ignorant believers is to be extended later in the novel.

Hermann Goering Division Hermann Goering, one of Hitler's major henchmen and leaders, was Head of the Luftwaffe (Air Force) in the Second World War.

a superhuman ping-pong player There is considerable irony here, since 'recreation' consists of playing games (basketball, shooting skeet, pitching horseshoes) all of which seem to Heller to bring out a nasty competitive feeling in men, which sometimes erupts into killer rage – as it does with Orr in his attack on Appleby.

busted Colonel Moodus on the nose The whole of this sequence should be read for its *farcical* effect, but there is a serious note: the men are there to fight a war, but the chain reaction makes them aggressive when they are supposed to be relaxing. The 'war' of man's nature is as terrible as the war itself – another aspect of the 'enemy within' theme.

publicity releases i.e. pictures showing what this section of the air force was doing.

'Why?' ... 'Why not?' Note the superb, economic sick humour of Chief White Halfoat's response.

metamorphosis Transformation.

extrovert ... introvert Behaviour states, the first outward, uninhibited; the second withdrawn, secretive.

heebie-jeebies i.e. scared him, made him quake or tremble.

still outside the pale i.e. not accepted by the men.

the seeds of rancour ... took root Metaphorical natural image – but Heller is dealing rather cynically here with human nature.

he believed that all men were created equal Cathcart doesn't believe this at all, as he is to demonstrate. Remember Orwell's classic rendering in *Animal Farm* when he has the dictatorship of Napoleon pronounce that 'some are more equal than others'.

Chapter 7, McWatt

Yossarian's pilot, card-player and hummer of show tunes. Yossarian's conversation with Milo, and his determination to keep his supposed liver condition as bad as possible as a means of dodging flying. Milo is the mess officer, already deep in the selling and buying which is to make him celebrated and looked up to wherever he goes. There is also the ludicrous return of a half a bed-sheet to McWatt.

The main emphasis here is on the bent commercial activities of Milo, with inverted logic again one of the main themes of the chapter. Notice that the focus on characters and what they represent is seen always in the Catch-22 situation in which everyone finds himself.

buying eggs for seven cents apiece and selling them for five cents A further send-up of the profit motive, here satirical against big business, and perhaps underlining the failure-success theme that runs throughout the novel.

it couldn't be better ... without being worse Yossarian frequently uses antithesis and word-play to underline what he is getting at.

syndrome A set of concurrent symptoms in disease.

black market A term used in wartime to describe the illegal selling of goods, often rationed goods which were in short supply. Military involvement in such activities was common, and the activities of Milo are a satirical account of such involvement.

'Aardvaark's my name ... game' The cliché rhyme indicates the conventional nature of Aarfy – but see what Aarfy does later.

Philistines Uncultured people, those whose tastes are materialistic.

incapable of subtlety or guile, an honest frank face The whole description of Milo is ironic, underlining the idea that there is a marked difference between appearance and the reality of character. Heller may well be mocking the conventional novelist who seldom differentiates between the outward and inward person, in order to produce a composite expression of goodness or of evil.

even sell it at a high profit instead of giving it away Milo always has an eye for the main chance.

the syndicate This is Milo's 'sharing' ploy, high sounding but existing in his imagination, and to be used to 'buy' people in. This section is very much a satire on buying and selling, and the acquisitive, profiteering motives by which so many of us are ruled.

Chapter 8, Lieutenant Scheisskopf

Ironically, this swift-to-rise, limited officer has a German name (which, incidentally, means 'Shit-head'). But first there is a description of Clevinger and his Harvard career. Heller is perhaps attacking a wide range of intellectuals when he says of Clevinger that, 'He knew everything about literature except how to enjoy it.' Scheisskopf is worried about his cadet parade; in fact he is obsessed by parades. His wife is frustrated (with him if not with others), and Scheisskopf himself hates Clevinger – the limited military 'bull' man and the intellectual are really on opposite sides. The interrogation of Clevinger is a fine parody of nonsense talk and nonsensical rules and decisions, the final one being that he has to walk 'fifty-seven punishment tours'.

Both Clevinger and Scheisskopf are caricatures of particular types. The marching sequence shows the emphasis on mechanical activity which is pointless in war and any situation but which passes for achievement. There is a delightful emphasis on sexual promiscuity – the 'release' for the men in wartime, but this is stale and mechanistic too in a sense. The court martial, with its totally rigid, inverted lines of logicality which focus in irrational hate, is a superb example of black comedy.

signing petitions, circulating petitions A satirical account of undergraduate life, the whole paragraph should be read with attention as it is ironically presenting the nature of university existence without academic disciplines.

empathy, Aristotle Again the satire is evident – all the things mentioned are 'vogue' interests, that is, it would be considered to be 'with it' if you talked about any of these. Aristotle (385–322 BC), the great law-giving philosopher, his works covered vast areas of speculation.

like a beardless Lear A reference to the tragic king in Shakespeare's *King Lear*.

R.O.T.C. Reserve Officers' Training Corps.

Dori Duz A very obvious pun, exploited to the full in the description of the 'lively little tart' Yossarian loves. There is a running irony on sexual licentiousness throughout *Catch-22*, thought it would be idle to pretend there is a moral tone about the irony!

mathematics major i.e. her main subject studied at university.

Such men were dangerous The phrase is an echo of *Julius Caesar*, Act I, Scene 2: Caesar's appraisal of Cassius, who had 'a lean and hungry look'. Here Scheisskopf is thinking of Clevinger.

It could not be anything to do with the parades ... A fine satirical sequence ridiculing the military obsession with show and marching as distinct from practical, useful, preparation for battle activity. Yossarian compares the parades to the achievements of Olympic athletes, where winners 'had done something of no benefit to anyone more capably than everyone else'.

Krafft-Ebing The German neurologist who wrote on psychology and sexual matters (1840–1902).

Leonardo's exercises in anatomy A reference to Leonardo da Vinci (1452–1519) whose talents covered a wide range of cultural and scientific activity.

titanic struggles for the unattainable High-flown language which in fact negates his ambitions, by exposing his complete lack of perspective.

nailing the twelve men ... to a long two-by-four beam This is farcical, ridiculous, but the satire is directed at those who put petty achievement before humanity.

nickel-alloy swivels Almost as if they are toy soldiers, as indeed they are in Scheisskopf's mind – like the ones he secretly buys.

mores Customs or conventions.

the impressive fainting ceremony A ridiculing of the fact that men faint at big parades, and a suggestion that this aspect has been deliberately incorporated into the ritual.

epochal i.e. epoch-making, outstanding. The invention of 'swingless marching' is so ridiculous as to need no comment here, but it is clear that Scheisskopf will be promoted for this worthless idea.

a true military genius Here the irony is direct and uncompromising: stigmatizing the nature of promotion, and what you have to do to get it.

schmuck Yiddish word for a 'fall guy', an idiotic fellow.

Who gives a damn about parades? Lieutenant Engle's is the voice of reason: he is far more interested in sexual perversion than in the boredom of routine – a sick joke.

The Officer defending him was Lieutenant Scheisskopf The ridiculous composition of the Action Board – with prosecution and defender dependent upon Scheisskopf – is a satire on military tribunals and their composition generally.

they threw the book i.e. charged him with everything.

Solomon Islands Islands in the Pacific.

'No, sir I ...' The whole of this exchange, and of others in this chapter, depends for its humour upon slapstick nonsense and good timing, like a cross-talk comedians' act. By the end, however, the whole thing becomes reminiscent of an interrogation, with no chance of the truth being discovered – and no wish to discover it.

Popinjay A lightweight, but conceited person.

shit creek ... without Current slang in wartime meaning 'There's no hope for you'.

'Justice is a knee in the gut ...' A superb account of what justice is *not* – a classic misdefinition of violence – underhand and final.

They would have lynched him ... 'They're after everybody' Another underlining of the 'enemy within', the blind actions of men in power and how they affect, reduce, those under them.

Chapter 9, Major Major Major Major

An account of his birth, career, unimpressiveness and resemblance to Henry Fonda. Some account, too, of his father's life and Major Major's becoming a 'flagrant nonconformist' – which means that he conforms to everything. Having established what he most needs – friendly relations with the men – he is appalled when he is promoted through no merit of his own. He compensates by firstly signing Washington Irving's name to documents, then later John Milton's, then reversing them. He tries to get back into the basketball games, is beaten up, then eats alone and rarely sees anybody. Yossarian does get through to him, but cannot get any ruling.

The tracing of this ridiculous non-career is another essay in black humour, with the classical outsider given the promotion that ensures he will remain an outsider. Since he is really a conformist, this is a terrible punishment, with guilt and uncertainty attending all he does, or rather doesn't do. There is a keen edge too in the notion that promotion leads to jealousy and rejection, the meaninglessness of documents which are countermanded and useless anyway, and the ineptitude of the C.I.D. men who fail to find the culprit who is before them. There is the grotesque humour of the leaps through the window – again the visual effect – and of the fears and disappearance of Captain Flume.

Minniver Cheevy From the celebrated poem by Edward Arlington Robinson (1869–1935).

He filled out the birth certificate without faltering A parody of the strong silent man – and also the opposite of the 'conventional' anxious father image.

like a desiccated old vegetable Again, an anti-romantic comment on childbirth.

moiling A muddy sky is implied.

Some men are born mediocre, some men achieve mediocrity A straight parody of Malvolio's inflated self-praise in *Twelfth Night* (Act III, Scene 4) which is itself an echo of the faked letter in Act II, Scene 5: 'Some are born great . . .'

three strikes on him i.e. against him. In American baseball, after the 'batter' misses the ball three times ('three strikes') he is 'out'.

alfalfa Clover-like plant used for fodder.

at the crack of noon Simple parody of the commonly used 'crack of dawn'.

A & P Atlantic & Pacific – a chain of food stores operating throughout the United States.

They told him to look before he leaped This and the following show the cliché advice given to us when we are young, and Heller caps these with the dramatic reversal of standards – the teaching to kill (in wartime) which upsets our previous conditioning.

flagrant nonconformist i.e. he never did any of the things (like committing adultery) that they did.

'What's the matter with American history' Parody of loud patriotism.

'Who promoted Major Major?' Satire against politicians who have nothing better to do than to raise minor criticisms.

like Saul The first king of Israel (Samuel 10,21,24).

mimeograph Another word for the duplicating machine which, before the advent of photocopying was (and still is, to a lesser extent) used for taking copies of material typed on stencils.

He had been plagued by one extra major The satire here is directed against the compulsive military need for numbers (not people) to be exactly right.

a reef of curious, reflective faces Frequently the language in *Catch-22* is unobtrusively poetic.

Most of the official documents that came to Major Major's desk did not concern him at all This statement, and the rest of the paragraph, is an ironic attack on the capacity of the military to proliferate useless information to which nobody pays any attention, just to show that something is being done – though to what purpose nobody knows.

Procrastination is the Thief of Time Another cliché proverb, like the one that follows it, supposed to keep up morale and standards.

Orvieto The place is unimportant, but the reference to the dead man in Yossarian's tent is clarified in the next few sentences.

'He's a lot cleverer than we thought' The whole of the dialogue involving each of the CID men and Major Major is a parody of the detective deducing facts in the films. Here of course it involves a general standard of idiocy on the part of the CID men and, of course, false deductions. The whole episode is *farcical*. This is enhanced (as General Peckem would say) by the *slapstick* nature of the constant jumping through the window. The technique is not unlike that employed in the silent films.

hightailing i.e. fleeing.

with purple gums Remember that this is part of standard practice for Gus and Wes.

John Milton (1608–1674) The author of the epic poem *Paradise Lost*, the title of which has an ironic application here.

'Is anybody in the John, Milton?' A pun – 'the John' is American slang for 'the lavatory'.

Great Loyalty Oath Crusade Again, a satirical attack, this time against the creation of useless and time-consuming activities in the false name of patriotism.

Maine lobsters ... an important member of the French underground
A fine contrast between the luxurious food and the man who has been
fighting for his country in German-occupied Paris. The contrast is also
between black-market profiteering and human sacrifice – beneath the
farce and the flippancy, Heller always keeps an eye on the seriousness
of the war – often, as with the re-iteration of Snowden's death,
establishing in the reader's consciousness a sense of perspective on the
suffering.

dewberry A kind of blackberry, a bramble.

taking off all his clothes after the Avignon Although there is a farcical
element in Yossarian naked on parade, there is also a poignant truth
in his gesture – the wish to stand cleansed of Snowden's insides,
cleansed of war. There is a terrible irony that he is there to receive a
medal.

They jumped inside the office Once more the switch is away from
suffering to farce – almost a protection against it.

**Some people are getting killed and a lot more are making money and
having fun** *Catch-22* endorses this statement, and all wars endorse it
too.

Chapter 10, Wintergreen

This deals with the disappearance of Clevinger, the influence of
Wintergreen and his regular demotions, Appleby's atttempt to
see Major Major, and the spreading fear of death among the
squadron. The joke about the dead man continues, and the
emphasis is on death and the siege of Bologna.

AWOL Absent without official leave.

go over the hill To absent oneself without leave from a military unit.

like the morning in Pianosa seven months later The movement of
Catch-22 is almost circular, and clues like this indicate Heller's
'scrambling' of time: this technique can produce a nightmare effect.

Atabrine A proprietary brand of quinacrine, a drug used to combat
malaria. The Splendid Atabrine Insurrection was an attempt to lower
their own health standards by refusing to take it. Here the Major
Major farce of never seeing anybody is played again, this time with the
urgent and earnest Appleby.

shards and Hepplewhite furniture The first, beetles, the second a
celebrated and delicate style of furniture owing its name to the
craftsman who died in 1786.

He was simply a replacement pilot The final explanation of the dead
man in Yossarian's tent, but note the narrative art of Heller who, by
mentioning the man several times without telling us the full story, has
kept us in a state of suspense. Several other incidents are treated in the
same way in the course of the novel.

Mudd Ironically, deliberately chosen name, with a commonplace pun involved.

the unknown soldier Very ironic paragraph; this soldier was *really* unknown, even to his comrades.

the moldy odor of mortality The whole sequence is from Yossarian's consciousness, and marks the fear of death.

like a melancholy buzzard Notice how the image immediately relates to the atmosphere of death and apprehension.

backing up in protest . . . smells like a charnel house Reference to decaying waste matter and to a vault where dead bodies and bones are piled. It looks forward, in terms of physical revulsion and horror, to Yossarian's surrealistic walk through Rome later.

Revision questions on Chapters 1–10

1 Indicate the part played by the Chaplain in these chapters.

2 Give an account of three incidents which you find grotesque and/or amusing in Chapters 1–6.

3 Write an essay on the obsessions of any two characters in these chapters. Refer closely to the text in your answer.

4 Compare and contrast any two characters in these chapters.

5 In what ways is Yossarian the central character so far? Refer closely to the text to support your views.

Chapter 11, Captain Black

The latter is sadistically delighted about the coming attack on Bologna. Black had expected to succeed Major Duluth as squadron commander, and it is he who spreads the rumour that Major Major is really Henry Fonda. He originates the Loyalty Oath Crusade with its succession of meaningless signatures and parades culminating in the singing of four choruses of the Star Spangled Banner. The resultant inefficiency is stopped when the leonine Major—de Coverley requests food.

In addition to the send up of the Loyalty Oath Crusade, there is the fact that it delays combat mission preparations, in other words there is method in this kind of madness. The theme is that routines have to be established although they are pointless – always in the forces one has to be seen to be doing something. The lack of any kind of coordination between the officer groups is evident. The common denominator of fear is always used –

you must conform, whether it is an oath or a fight. Heller employs brilliant contrast between what Major—de Coverley appears and what he actually is. The appearance and reality theme is again the major concern in the novel. War, patriotism are both trenchantly deglamorized.

Eat your livers i.e. suffer. Black is a sadist.

he was a Communist Remember that *Catch-22* contains topical references to the early fifties in America, the era of McCarthyism (1956–1963) and the witch-hunting of those who had been members, no matter how far back, of the Communist party.

a loyalty oath . . . a second loyalty . . . a third loyalty oath This description is satirical, attacking that aspect of military life which consists of 'signing' for things and going through a time-consuming and inefficient ritual to get them.

The Star-Spangled Banner The national anthem of the United States. The words, by Francis Scott Key, were written during the bombardment of Fort McHenry in September 1814. The tune is from an English song, 'To Anacreon in Heaven'.

the combat men . . . dominated by the administrators Heller is recording a fact of any organization, that there is a hierarchy controlling the destiny of its underlings. Here the irony is that the combat men – those who actually fight – should be more valued than the administrators.

signing, pledging and singing The farcical element of the crusade is emphasized here.

'it's going to look mighty funny to the F.B.I.' Black is not loath, as we see from this, to use blackmail.

Chapter 12, Bologna

Mission delayed through rain, the city supposedly captured by troops, Yossarian alters the bomb line, General Peckem gets the medal, but there is a drunken night out for Yossarian, Chief White Halfoat and others in Colonel Black's stolen car. This farcical sequence ends with Hungry Joe trying to shoot Huple's cat and Yossarian rescuing the cat and setting up a fight between it and Hungry Joe – but the cat won't fight. There is an undercurrent of hysteria running through the chapter, almost as if it is a reaction from combat.

The medal award is another direct comment – those who get them are part of the farce of competition for undeserved promotion. The cat incident looks forward to the killing of Hungry Joe. The hysteria referred to above is an important atmospheric indicator which is present in most of the novel, and is registered in sick farce, fear and the reiterations and reverberations of death.

All through the night . . . saddened by the stars i.e. because they can see them and know that it is not raining, and that therefore they may have to take off. The first few words are the echo of the traditional Welsh song which dwells on the security of God – an ironic echo here.

incubating in each man hatched into hatred A simile from animal nature to underline the stress the men are under.

'Do you think we're bombing our own troops now?' Ironic in view of Milo's exploit.

Egyptian cotton . . . Zippo lighters Obviously the black market is providing opportunities for men of initiative.

a buck apiece A dollar each.

'The enemy . . . is anybody who's going to get you killed;' Almost the key to the novel, and certainly an underlining of the 'enemy within' theme.

But Clevinger did forget it, and now he was dead Note another switch in the time sequence, very clever, since death comes suddenly in wartime, and he who was living dies – and we as readers feel the impact when a character we know well is taken from us, not by the strict chronological sequence, but with the sudden wrenching of time which approximates to wartime death.

like tongueless wraiths with cigarettes Ghostly effect – and the irony is that they symbolize the ghosts of the dead; others just like themselves.

It glues a whole formation of planes together in mid-air A sick joke: men in fear will resort to the grotesque, by way of laughing it off.

'Rain, rain go a—' The nursery song. Ironically, the rain does stop at this point, just when the men don't want it to.

'Pass the salt, Walt . . . Shoot me a beet, Pete . . .' Simple rhyming speech, boring to those whose wit is more sophisticated.

'Fists, fangs and claws' A fine farcical sequence. Heller is of course satirizing people who talk to animals as though they can understand the actual words.

Chapter 13, Major—de Coverley

He flies to Florence, is always seen to be first in entering captured cities, and is an enigma to American and German Intelligence. His entry into Rome is described, though here he is wounded in the eye by a flower thrown by an 'intoxicated' old man. Yossarian is awarded a medal for flying twice over the target in the incident in which Kraft is killed.

The grotesquerie continues with Major—de Coverley flying to Florence, but the real focus is on the incompetence of either side's military intelligence to find out who he is. The send up of sexual promiscuity also continues with the maid who is always accessible, the send-up of black marketeering with the officers gorging Milo's supplies. Inefficiency as a label is the fear which the top brass are determined to reduce, hence Yossarian's decoration.

lithe young infantrymen with carbines ... or fell dead in doorways Heller's sense of cinema never deserts him, and here he is 'sending up' the kind of film Hollywood would be making at the time in celebration of the 'glorious' American victories.

would put out i.e. would make themselves (sexually) available.

Gargantuan appetites Gargantua was a gigantic personage in Rabelais's (1483–1553) satire of that name; he had an immense appetite and lived for several centuries.

she laid for everybody By now we are used to the reversal of standards, and understand the humour behind the term 'virtuous' applied to the maid with 'lime-coloured panties'.

the bald-headed girl in Sicily She is referred to several times in *Catch-22*, an example of Heller's use of the repeated grotesque incident.

excoriating laugh Strictly, with part of the skin removed – a vivid way of describing one thing in terms of another.

Spartan i.e. very brave (ironic here), derived from the Spartan warriors who bravely defended the pass of Thermopylae.

colossus Statue of much more than life size, conceived, like the Colossus of Rhodes, as standing astride dominions.

like a Big Ten fullback A reference to American football.

'Malta's not so far away' As will be seen from much of this, Major—de Coverley does not listen: he merely repeats his thoughts aloud. There is some clever speech parody in these exchanges.

The smell of a fresh egg snapping exotically Fine irony underlining the petty as distinct from the important.

the Po i.e. the river flowing through Ferrara.

tiny metal fragments began tap dancing Not a good image, but one which captures the flavour of the Hollywood musical of the time, when tap-dancing (witness Fred Astaire) was still the vogue.

for they had all died in the distance of a mute and secluded agony A poignant piece of realism, emphasizing perspective and the nature of suffering, which is beneath all the surface humour of this anti-war novel.

And let's promote him to captain Again the terrible irony is apparent – a cynical appraisal of the way in which medals are won or rather given – for to some, war is a game, a question of manipulation in order to retain some small power.

Chapter 14, Kid Sampson

The turning back from the raid on Bologna – doubly ironic in view of Yossarian's supposed bravery in the previous chapter. Yossarian is in charge and affects not to be able to hear on the intercom. Later he goes back to the beach and sees the other planes returning. There had been no defences at Bologna.

The simple irony plays over the whole operation, since no defences shows that once more military intelligence has been at fault. Yossarian's reaction as he hears the planes returning is hysterical because of what he has done, but there is also some relief in it.

like a shivering turkey buzzard A slight but significant alteration to the earlier image of Doc – but remember that he is a hypochondriac.
occlusion Closure, obstruction.
The breeze rustled leaves in a dry and diaphanous distance There is some poetic writing in this sequence, a little-noticed aspect of Heller's style.
he saw dozens of new mushrooms . . . poking their nodular fingers . . . like lifeless stalks of flesh . . . necrotic profusion One of the finest pieces of writing in the novel. Yossarian is highly sensitive and imaginative, often seeing things with a surrealistic and nightmare intensity. The growth is, ironically and terrifyingly, symbolic of death; the increasing numbers of the dead in war. This symbol is followed by one of purifying, as Yossarian bathes in the sea and then sleeps. These two pages (156–7) should be studied in some detail by the reader, for they display the fineness of Heller's style, his ability to write symbolically and at the same time to capture the vagaries of the imagination and the transformation of mood. There are moments like this, moments of high seriousness, scattered throughout *Catch-22*, which give the quicksilver of the satire a firm base of humanity and compassion.

Chapter 15, Piltchard & Wren

'Nothing so wonderful as war had ever happened to them before.' This short chapter describes the complementary pair above, and also the bombing of Bologna. When Yossarian discovers that Orr is also on the mission, he realizes why so much flak has been attracted to them. Yossarian packs in order to go to Rome. Notice that Aarfy, who does not lose his nerve, is regarded as insane by Yossarian, another reversal of what would normally be thought.

'that's all I'm going to say to you on the subject' Fine irony which once again reflects the fact that people don't listen to what is said.

to paste i.e. bomb heavily.

like a fat lazy fly Note how the simile contrasts with the real menace in the air.

twin spires of flak Again, the metaphor – almost a spiritual one – contrasts with the terrible reality of the fire.

orbicular Spherical, globular.

'Get back in the ship' i.e. the plane.

with the feeling of warm slime Note the way in which physical discomfort is described by way of revolting physical sensation.

ululating Howling, hooting.

moue Pout.

like an eerie ogre in a dream The simile fits in with much of Yossarian's experience, which is of a nightmarish or surrealistic quality.

its vivid pyre A heap of combustible material.

feathered i.e. broken, shattered, in strips.

Chapter 16, Luciana

Yossarian takes Luciana to a black-market restaurant, then to the bus depot, before returning lustfully to the restaurant. Yossarian also covets the Countess and her daughter. When he gets back to the apartment, Aarfy is there but without the blonde in whom Yossarian is interested. Next morning Luciana arrives, tidies up, then gets into bed with Yossarian; but shortly afterwards they are interrupted by Hungry Joe, who races off to get his camera. Luciana gives Yossarian her name and address, which he stupidly tears up, though he later goes in search of her.

After the leave in Rome, with the various reactions and the sordid equation of sex and money, Yossarian comes back to the terrible reality of Pianosa and the fact that Colonel Cathcart has raised the number of missions to 40. The definition of Catch-22 permeates the whole novel. At the risk of repetition, one must say that it is the war, from which there is no escape, whether you are being killed or selling your body.

Anzac Australian and New Zealand Army Corps.

jitterbug Dance popular at the beginning of the war and during it, at the time considered rather daring.

lively, chirping, attractive girls ... flushed and merry proprietors The language is a parody of the romantic, sentimental style of description. Note also Luciana's scar – the war scars everybody, as we see in *The Eternal City* chapter. Luciana's scar stimulates Yossarian's compassion.

'Capisci?' Do you understand?

'Cosa vuol dire?' What does it mean?

that wonderful tomato i.e. beautiful girl.

'Come?' What?

'Subito' Quickly.

The snarling vituperation of unshaven bus drivers Notice how this sequence is in deliberate contrast with the sequence about the restaurant.

fructified i.e. made fruitful.

cabalistic i.e. mystical, occult.

'Vive com' un animale!' (He) lives like an animal!

'finito!' Finished!

'Dove?' Where?

'Perche non posso sposare?' Why can't I get married? (The remainder of the dialogue in Italian can easily be followed here.)

'Carina, ti amo' Darling, I love you.

stopped on a dime i.e. at once (in a space as small as a ten-cent piece).

Multi *dinero*, Much money. (Probably Hungry Joe's faulty attempt at Italian.)

like a floundering frog Heller is fond of varying his style, sometimes, as here, including simple images from nature which contrast with his unusual choice of words at other times.

another hump i.e. had slept with her again.

her long, lithe, nude, young vibrant limbs into tiny pieces of paper A superb transference, for the address *is* Luciana in the sense that without the address he will not see her again.

unperjured friendship i.e. because there is nothing false about it, no lies; it is merely animal sexuality.

Chapter 17, The soldier in white

Yossarian and his periodic retreats into hospital. There are fewer deaths in hospital than there are outside, and the dignity of death in hospital is compared with that of death in war. There is gossip about the soldier in white who never makes a sound, though the Texan talks to him, and nurse Cramer is fond of him; then they discover him dead, and we realize that another time-shift has occurred in the unravelling of the novel – we have gone back to where we started. Yossarian is obsessed that everyone is out to kill him, and makes a plea to Doc Daneeka to ground him.

An important chapter structurally, since there is much explanation of Yossarian when we realize that we are at the beginning and that retrospect, of various degrees and with varying narrative emphases, has dominated the previous chapters. In other words, the psychology, both individual and composite of war and its effects, has been examined. Yossarian marvels that he has survived for twenty-eight years since everything in life is intent on his death.

hernias and hemorroids i.e. ruptures, and haemorrhoids (Eng. sp.) – what are commonly called 'piles'.

They didn't take it on the lam Read the whole of this paragraph for an appraisal of death in the sanity of comfort as distinct from death in the insanity of war.

like an alpaca sack full of hairy strawberry ice cream, bleeding, pink toes awry The comparison conveys with terrible actuality, despite its nature, the finality of death – the complete lack of life, the loss of living motion.

kept him spick and span The irony is that it is his *outside* they keep clean – his inside is obviously beyond hygiene.

leviathan The sea monster, hence 'monstrous' here.

the *Hippolytus* of Euripedes . . . Theseus Famous Greek tragic dramatist (480–406BC), Euripides wrote a number of plays, including the one named here, some eighteen of which have survived. Theseus is the legendary Greek hero who slew the Minotaur, and ranks second only to Hercules in heroic legend.

goldbrick Sham.

Tojo Japanese wartime leader who caused his country to enter the war with the attack on the United States at Pearl Harbor.

lackeys i.e. servants, those working for others (the implication here is that they were hired to kill).

to catch and coddle a cancer cell Notice the poetic alliteration, which ironically conceals the seriousness with which Heller is writing.

Ewing's tumor A tumour that invades the shaft of a long bone, tends to recur, but rarely spreads.

doctors are cleaning up i.e. making money.

Chapter 18, The soldier who saw everything twice

Yossarian in hospital for observation. Doctors are further satirized over the use/non-use of the ice-bag, and Yossarian finds himself in quarantine pending the investigation of another patient. A jump forward in time to Yossarian's spending the next Thanksgiving Day with Dori Duz, and his attack on God which so upsets her. Back to the present, with Yossarian, in imitation of another patient, pretending to see everything twice.

The patient dies, and in a sick sequence involving a parody of the death-bed scene, the parents arrive and are persuaded into mistaking Yossarian for their dead son, Giuseppi.

There is both pathos and poignancy in this chapter operating beneath the level of the sick joke. The idea that doctors can be conned by malingerers but that there are genuine (perhaps neuresthenic) cases as well is also evident.

intern Advanced student or recent graduate, residing in hospital and acting as assistant physician or surgeon.

a country bumpkin This paragraph is an ironic attack on the Christian concept of a benign God – Yossarian argues that the incidences of pain and suffering are too great and he comes to the conclusion that God is a blunderer. It is one of the most cynical sequences in the book, but difficult to refute logically. Scheisskopf's wife is reduced to saying 'the God I don't believe in is a good God, a just God'.

'We made him all better.' A fine economic send-up of medical complacency based on ignorance.

'We're all in this business of illusion together.' Another cynical aside on the medical profession.

tacky Difficult, sticky.

sere Withered, dried up.

umber Natural pigment like ochre but darker and browner.

'His name is Yossarian, Pa,' This section involves a black comedy of mistaken identity, but the underlying theme is perhaps that when we are dying we don't need to be watched over. There is a further implication that people go through the motions of doing the right thing, even when this involves talking nonsense.

lying in her lap like fallen moths Again, the sudden truth of observation – Heller even in the middle of a grotesque scene like this, is capable of fine figurative observation.

Chapter 19, Colonel Cathcart

All the latter's contradictions are described, both physical and mental. There is his relationship with Colonel Korn, and his wish, inspired by reading the *Saturday Evening Post*, to have prayers before briefing meetings. But when Cathcart gets down to detail he wants God cut out of the prayers, and can't bear the thought of enlisted men attending the prayers (of 1½ minutes' duration if held). He is an unmitigated snob, saying 'Some of my best friends are enlisted men', but it is a hollow remark. He abandons the prayer project, and when the chaplain complains about the sixty missions the men have to fly at this stage he observes, in relation to Yossarian, 'Tell him to trust in God.'

A subtle continuation of the 'god' theme of the previous chapter, with an overt comment on paranoia and an opportunist definition of hypocrisy. Cathcart represents ambition and the wish for publicity, but he is on shifting sands as regards status. His selfishness is yet another example of the reduction of humanity.

sarcophagus Stone coffin, usually adorned with inscription.

'Black Eyes' ... **'Feathers in My Cap'** The column headings written by Colonel Cathcart define the extremes of his moods: his slights and successes, imagined rather than real.

The Saturday Evening Post American magazine with a world circulation and a certain prestige – hence Cathcart's interest.

bushels of red plum tomatoes Evidence of the black market activity of Cathcart and Korn.

Zion The south-western hill of Jerusalem which David took; it was called 'the city of David'.

'I'd like to keep away from the subject of religion altogether if we can.' A fine stroke of irony to indicate Cathcart's basic ignorance and at the same time his unscrupulousness and ambition.

'a much nicer aerial photograph when the bombs explode close together' Note the emphasis here, which is not on achievement but on the effect created, thus revealing a petty and unconcerned attitude towards suffering and dying.

'a minute and a half for you in the schedule' The time shows just how much importance Cathcart attaches to the spiritual sustenance of the men in his command.

'Atheism is against the law' This is a merciless exposure of the ignorance, the blinkered attitude of Cathcart.

'They've got a God and a chaplain of their own' His snobbery again, but later the interrogators of the chaplain won't believe that anyone like Cathcart could make such a statement.

'It isn't that I think the enlisted men are dirty, common and inferior.' The reverse technique applies again, for that is exactly what he does think.

'My sister is an enlisted man' i.e. has joined the forces, but there is an element of innuendo here that is followed up in the next statement and makes Cathcart suspicious.

Chapter 20, Corporal Whitcomb

The chaplain and his sense of failure stressed, with a description of Colonel Korn and his hatred of the chaplain. The chaplain lives in the woods with his assistant Corporal Whitcomb, who is also contemptuous of him. On this occasion when he returns he sees the corporal talking to someone in hospital clothes; there is an argument between the chaplain and Whitcomb, and the chaplain's feelings of *déjà vu* are stressed. The discussion with Whitcomb reveals to us that the question of Washington Irving's signature is still unresolved. (Remember Yossarian's writing it, then Major Major's adopting the idea.)

Again there is an emphasis on the pettiness of administration to the exclusion of humanity. There is also the reversal of rank and power in view of the studied insubordination of Whitcomb, and the irony of the chaplain's presence in the woods away from headquarters and hence unable to influence the men. This is the opposite of what should be happening.

Father Deliberate irony – in fact insulting, further showing in what little respect the chaplain is held.

How are things in the wilderness By Christian association, one is reminded of Christ's forty days in the wilderness – here it is again contemptuous of the chaplain to consign him to it in the first place.

rotunda Building of circular ground plan, usually with a dome.

disjuncted Separated.

sounds of revelry traveled to him at night The echo is of Byron's *Childe Harold* ('There was a sound of revelry by night') – the section dealing with the eve of the battle of Waterloo (1815).

afflatus Divine impulse or inspiration.

Déjà vu An important aspect of the novel – 'the feeling of having been there before', perhaps in some other life, is part of our experience. But it has a terrible and ironic significance in *Catch-22* not merely for the chaplain, but for the others and particularly Yossarian, for on every mission, with every death, they *have* experienced it before in a certain sense.

a Milky Way and a Babe Ruth Two well-known American chocolate bars containing caramel, nuts etc.

Revision questions on Chapters 11–20

1 Show how *Catch-22* operates at different levels in the action or situations of these chapters.

2 Indicate how conflict between characters influences the decisions in these chapters.

3 Write on one of the following: (i) the Glorious Loyalty Oath Crusade or (ii) Luciana or (iii) Major de—Coverley.

4 Write an essay on the character and career of Milo.

5 What do you find the most vivid incident in these chapters?
Write a detailed account of it, referring closely to the text.

Chapter 21, General Dreedle

The recollection of Yossarian standing naked in the ranks of the
medal ceremony, and Cathcart recalling him as the bombardier
to whom he awarded a medal! There are descriptions of Cathcart and his lonely nights in the farmhouse, his obsession with
Yossarian; a reference to Milo's bombing of his own men (details
later); then a description of General Dreedle, his nurse, and his
relationship with his son-in-law Colonel Moodus, and the latter's
enforced repression. Then we return to the naked Yossarian on
parade; his falling in love with the general's nurse; the complete
embarrassment of Cathcart; and the famous 'moaning
sequence', with Major Danby ordered to be shot by the General.
Moodus points out that this cannot be done, and Korn takes
over the briefing, convinced that he is making a good impres-
sion; later he learns from Cathcart that Dreedle has observed
that Korn makes him sick.

This is a brilliant study in power and neurotic interaction.
Remember that although the novel is set in wartime, Heller is
writing with the hindsight of the McCarthyite attacks on
Communists in high places, and the Cathcart obsession with
Yossarian has him arbitrarily associated with Communism and
Fascism. Again the incipient hysteria which lies behind so much
farce is present.

Yossarian! . . . 'Moaning (epidemic of during Avignon briefing)' This
    shows the way in which Cathcart's mind works – he is determined to
    incriminate Yossarian, blame him for everything, and links him
    deliberately with the words he italicized earlier – e.g. *subversive,
    Communist.*
the most tangible achievement he had going for him And this –
    forcing his men to fly more missions – is a vicious circle; he has to go
    on doing it, and the novel is largely concerned with the debilitating
    effect this has on the fliers – Yossarian, Dunbar, Dobbs and others.
Ivy League Group of universities and colleges in north-eastern USA,
    but the term is often used to describe their standards, attitudes,
    fashions in dress.
like haloes of bacon fat A superb combination of the visually
    grotesque.

croupy with a sharp cough.

K.P. Kitchen Police, i.e. a fatigue, preparing vegetables, cleaning up.

A man ... bled all over him This is of course Snowden, though the details do not emerge in full until late in the novel – part of Heller's technique in maintaining our suspense, and also, by repeating parts regularly in Yossarian's consciousness, to show what a deep effect this has had on him.

to wear neckties on the combat missions The satire here is directed at the ridiculous competitiveness between the military leaders to do something different and so score a point.

like a fertile oasis Good simile in view of the 'desert' in which the men find themselves situated.

confluences Coming together, uniting.

An elfin impulse possessed Nately Even he joins in – this is a slapstick sequence, funny in terms of sound and effect, both visual and auditory. I suppose the highlight is when Major Danby himself moans inadvertently.

'Take him out and shoot him.' Positively the most direct statement of 'the enemy within' – the ignorant military leader who assumes he has the power to take away the lives of those under him merely by issuing an order.

Neither had ever taken Major Danby outside and shot him before A subtle piece of humour, underlining the fact that in the forces you only do what you have done before – i.e. you never show any initiative.

'I think you'd better wait a minute, Dad' The last word holds the humour.

He was about to begin moaning aloud A deliberate stress of Cathcart's weakness, the way in which he swings from one extreme to the other.

rolling his eyes flirtatiously The tone shows that Korn, who is usually in calm control, is, like everyone else, sycophantic, sucking up to the General.

Chapter 22, Milo the Mayor

Natural return after this to the Snowden episode yet again, followed by a focus on Dobbs and his idea of murdering Cathcart for continually raising the number of missions they have to do. Brief account of Yossarian's and Orr's experiences with the prostitutes, followed by the egg-buying and chickpea account, with Milo's explanation of the working of the syndicate. When they get to Palermo Milo is treated by the populace as a hero (superb satire this) for he has succeeded in making Sicily one of the world's largest exporters of whisky. Later they fly off to Malta where Milo is Assistant Governor-General. The implication is that commercial success – or chicanery, or failure – can give you status, rank, celebrity. Milo's other positions are described – they are exotic – and the nature of the banana racket is indicated.

Beneath the farcical range of Milo's successes and titles there lies the indictment of the wartime profiteer. On one level this is hilarious narrative – again note the contrast with death and madness – but it is a very deliberate use of satire to indicate the nature of capitalism, the profit motive which dominates and conditions their lives.

like a trapped mouse The simple image is very effective – and it reminds us of Havermeyer's night-shooting in his tent.

like a pomaded pup tent Brilliantined hair, growing upwards to resemble a gable-shaped tent.

Cuban Panatella A type of cigar.

denudate skull i.e. she had no hair. The practice of shaving the heads of women who consorted with Germans in wartime was quite a common one.

that's what makes Sammy run i.e. that's what keeps things ticking over.

four-year-old pimp . . . eight-year-old virgins There is much sexual innuendo in *Catch-22*: here on the desirability of 'new' sexual experience, i.e. with, supposedly, very young girls.

The streets were jammed with joyous throngs The whole of this description is satirical – an attack on big business, on money making; for money is the god of all peoples regardless of their loyalties in war. Milo is to demonstrate this again and again, more particularly when he bombs his own men. But here the reception accorded a military conqueror is given to a monetary conqueror; the cynical implication is that Milo and his kind will always rule.

Tubas crumped Fine onomatopoeic effect of the noise made by that instrument.

trampled to death This reference points to the 'sick' humour of the occasion.

a hot-shot i.e. important.

the horse chestnuts were back in his mouth It is part of Orr's character *not* to reveal – just as he doesn't reveal his intentions.

Assistant Governor-General Milo's ranks show that you can buy anything with money – including titles, as we see on reading further.

Berber guards North African in origin.

the Sheik of Araby The ridiculous nature of Milo's titles is stressed by the addition of this one, which comes from the romantic popular song. Vice-Shah has the ring of falseness too, and the Caliph and the Imam, though real, have a strong *Arabian Nights* flavour which adds to the humour.

stock-ticker i.e. machine that records prices of stock.

piasters Piastres – small Turkish or Egyptian coins.

Chapter 23, Nately's Old Man

Nately's time is taken up with finding his whore again, and when they all go off to the large brothel Nately gets caught up in conversation with the disreputable old man who reminds him of his father 'because the two were nothing at all alike'. The old man is the timeless opportunist who lives for the moment, always supporting the current conquerors and thus surviving; he it was who hit Major—de Coverley in the eye with a flower. Nately's particular upbringing is described. After this his girl goes off street-walking, and Nately finds himself with the old man.

The old man is a genuine grotesque, but the nightmare innuendo is present here, and again, despite the comedy, there is a suggestion of Kafka. Nately, like each of the others – and this is a reflex of wartime experiences – has now acquired an obsession.

'We can even threaten to push them out the window.' This anticipates what Aarfy actually does.

cornucopia Goat's horn represented in art as overflowing with flowers, fruit and corn.

began to die Remember that Hungry Joe is always 'killed' when he is surrounded by female flesh.

like some satanic and hedonistic deity on a throne This adds to the grotesque nature of this chapter which, like some of the others in the novel, is not unlike the atmosphere created by Kafka, particularly in *The Castle* and *The Trial*.

otiose Lazy, leisured.

penny-ante Any game (of cards) in which the 'ante', or limit, is one cent. A small-stake business deal.

'The real trick lies in *losing* wars' The reverse of the currently held philosophy – but so much of *Catch-22* revels in the use of paradox.

Oberleutnant German officer.

even though they had both been very good to him Yossarian is implying that he has the reverse of normal reactions, that Nately is crazy because he hasn't any of the neuroses normal people have.

pushers i.e. who 'push' for money.

Vanderbilt . . . Rockefeller . . . Reynolds . . . Duke . . . Astor American families of millionaire status.

like a twig with the bark peeled off Vivid image from nature – from time to time Heller achieves a sudden poetic effect.

Brooks Brothers Superior US menswear suppliers.

Chapter 24, Milo

Milo and his trading successes, his acquisition of aircraft and his deals with the enemy, take up the first part of this chapter. He organizes attacks for both sides, for they are both members of the syndicate. Then M & M enterprises reaches the point of collapse after Milo's bulk purchase of Egyptian cotton; but he lands a contract with the Germans to bomb his own outfit. In the 'sickest' section of this novel his own men are bombed with nightmare effect and there is a great wave of anti-Milo feeling. However, when he reveals that the tremendous profit he has made is to be shared out equally, adding that the government should get out of the war and leave it all to private industry, he is forgiven. Again we revert to Yossarian and Snowden and the return from Avignon. The time switch has occurred again, with Yossarian deciding that he doesn't want to wear a uniform any more. He hides in a tree where he is found by Milo and both are moved as they watch the funeral of Snowden. But afterwards Milo becomes, inevitably, concerned with his cotton deal activities.

Money rules wars, and wars rule people. Bombing or killing your own side in error is a fact of war, but to do it as commercial profit – imposing money morality as a replacement for human morality – shows how far private enterprise can go. Milo ensures that it does.

a livelier iris gleamed upon the burnished dove A paraphrase of the line preceding 'In the spring a young man's fancy/Lightly turns to thoughts of love' (Tennyson's *Locksley Hall*).

pink paper panties i.e. nicely wrapped.

bursitis Inflammation of the pouch-like cavity between joints.

Liberia ... Karachi The place-names indicate the range of Milo's activities.

halvah A Turkish confection made from ground almonds and honey in flavour.

yams ... collards The first are edible tubers similar in flavour to sweet potatoes: the second a variety of cabbage that does not have a heart.

excoriating Removing skin by abrasion.

argosies Large merchant vessels (a poetic term).

Napoleons ... *petits fours* Confectionery.

Kugelhopf, pumpernickel and Pfefferkuchen ... Linzer ... Dobos Torten All indicate the range of Milo's Fancy Pastry and related 'cookies'.

Axis Sally's ... Lord Haw-Haw American and British traitors respectively, who broadcast regularly throughout the war, in an attempt to get allied soldiers to defect to the enemy.

apocalyptic Revelatory (in more ways than one it seems here).

banshee A spirit whose wail portends death in a house.

Strafe . . . It's in the contract i.e. go down and fire with your machine guns – we have to.

stentorian With a powerful voice. Named after Stentor, a Greek herald.

He could reimburse the government for all the people and property In human terms, of course he can't; Heller is saying that money is more important than lives, a further underlining of the immorality of war.

logy Drowsy, drugged.

'It's the tree of life' Very ironic, for Milo is quick to note that it is in fact a chestnut, and he sells chestnuts.

as inflexible as lumps of wood Down to earth image which contrasts realistically with the animation of Yossarian and Milo, the latter of course with business matters which concern them all.

Calvin Coolidge President of the United States from 1923 to 1928.

They're no better than a bunch of crooks How ironic that Milo, the skilled businessman and manipulator, should say this!

Chapter 25, The Chaplain

The chaplain, full of self-doubt, is brooding on his unpopularity. He discusses *déjà vu* with Yossarian. He thinks of his troubles at the Officers' club, his loving relationship with his wife, his sincerity and his inability to help anyone. Perhaps most of all he broods on his relationship with Corporal Whitcomb, who is always rude and impudent to him. He learns that Major Major has been to see him, but of course when he goes to see Major Major the latter isn't there. The Chaplain meets the man of the woods, Captain Flume, and they discuss Chief White Halfoat's threat. Next Cathcart sees the chaplain, who is appalled, about Whitcomb's standard letter of condolence – Cathcart's aim is to produce casualties (he mentions another raid on Avignon) so that he can get himself into the Christmas issue of the *Saturday Evening Post*. Dreedle sees the chaplain at the Officers' club and reprimands Cathcart yet again. The chaplain's own insecurity is made worse by the power struggle of his superior officers, in which he is used as a pawn.

savoir-faire Quickness to see and do the right thing.

ontology Department of metaphysics concerned with the essence, the being of things.

epistemological Theories of the methods or grounds of knowledge.

If they pricked him, didn't he bleed? And if he was tickled, didn't he laugh? The chaplain is an Anabaptist, not a Jew, but these lines are an echo of Shylock's moving speech in *The Merchant of Venice* (Act III, Scene 1). Heller continues to echo Shylock, and then updates the reference to include, for example, 'wounded by the same kind of weapons'.

the vision of the naked man in the tree Remember that the chaplain is given to imaginative impressions – his sight of Yossarian has given him a mystical sensation which he is doing his best to interpret in terms of his faith.

fossilized wooden ties i.e. hardened railway sleepers.

incarnadine Flesh-coloured, crimson.

ulcerated with rust ... color of poplar Further evidence of Heller's sudden poetically vivid writing.

hirsute specter i.e. hairy ghost-like creature.

canteen i.e. mess-tin.

lister bag i.e. containing chemically-treated drinking water.

Dear Mrs., Mr., Miss ... The letter of condolence is the finest example in the novel of the hypocrisy involved in such communications – and of their impersonality, and inadequacy, as expressions of feeling.

onyx-and-ivory riding crop An apt metaphor, since Cathcart is in fact flogging the chaplain with words.

getting lit i.e. 'lit up', drunk.

'The sooner we get some casualties ...' A terrible indictment of Cathcart and men like him – unscrupulous, sacrificing lives in order to further their own careers.

Ethan Frome The novel by Edith Wharton (1862–1937). It was published in 1911, and is uncharacteristic of her in the sense that it is based on a personal experience rather than being a novel of manners and society.

Chapter 26, Aarfy

Nately with his whore again, expressive of his love for her – and a sideways look at Aarfy as lead navigator, and his tendency to get them lost on missions. He cannot, or affects not to be able, to hear when they are flying, even when Yossarian is wounded. In hospital there is the usual joke sequence, this time about changing beds and changing identities.

Aarfy's capacity to get lost, and not to hear, seems to be symbolic of the effect war has had on him, that he shuts himself off from experience and only does what he wants to do – as he is to reveal in a terrible way later.

syrette A small syringe.

strawberry-strained . . . baritone buzz Note how the combination of
  colour and sound produces the 'fuzzy' feeling.
weevilled Weevils are beetles that feed on fruit, nuts, grain and
  cereals.
a fortiori To strength, strongly.

Chapter 27, Nurse Duckett

An account of Yossarian's first assault on her, and of Dunbar's
comic failure. There follows the interrogation of Yossarian by
Major Sanderson, the psychiatrist who is himself a mass of
complexes. There is a considered ridiculing of psychiatry in this
chapter with, inevitably, much emphasis on sex – and mistaken
identity too. Yossarian is told that he has a split personality and a
persecution complex. Dobbs tells how other pilots are being sent
home after flying only 45 missions; he further reveals his hatred
of Cathcart and his fear of flying any more missions. Sanderson
returns to tell Yossarian that he (Yossarian) is also a manic
depressive. Doc Daneeka brings the *terrible* news that in Europe
the Allies are winning – terrible because it means that they may
be all sent to the Pacific to fight the Japanese. Yossarian continues to insist that he is mad.

   The ridiculing of psychiatry doesn't prevent there being some
truth in what is discovered – Yossarian nearly gets away with it
here, since he is initially withdrawn from combat, but soon put
back on. It seems that the spiritual and the medical are equally
irrelevant. The continuation of the Pacific War is, of course,
Catch-22.

fulcrum The point against which the lever is placed.
Dunbar missed completely We are never far from slapstick comedy –
  and Dunbar's miss is just that.
agreeable and insincere A typical Heller paradox – but we meet with it
  often in life.
ambivalent attitude A cliché which, in terms of psychiatric diagnosis,
  means the co-existence of feelings of love and hate towards someone
  or something.
Purple Hearts Medal awarded for being in action, to members of the
  American armed forces during the Second World War.
keening Wailing, in a funereal tone.
manic-depressive Alternating between periods of elation and
  depression, sometimes with tendencies towards violence.
going to hell ever since we captured Paris Note once again the use of

paradox – instead of being delighted Doc sees the worst side, their possible removal to the Pacific.

Gothic line i.e. the German defences.

'I'm a licensed physician . . . Then keep your stupid licensed physician's mouth shut' Satire on the way we hide behind meaningless phrases that indicate a status not relevant to what is being discussed.

Chapter 28, Dobbs

Yossarian goes to Dobbs to re-introduce the subject of the killing of Cathcart; but Dobbs has nearly completed (so he thinks) the requisite number of missions. Meanwhile Orr has escaped death yet again, despite Milo's tampering with the life-jackets. Sergeant Knight tells the story of Orr's amazing resilience and adaptability, and, while Orr is repairing the stove, he is trying to tell Yossarian something – perhaps preparing him for his own desertion. Yossarian doesn't understand quite what Orr is implying. Yossarian certainly doesn't wish to fly with Orr, though the latter asks him to do so; Yossarian eats his heart out for his tent-mate when Orr fails to return from a mission.

A chapter full of irony since, as we shall see, what Orr is trying to communicate is of vital importance and could have changed everything for Yossarian. It is one of the tantalizing might-have-beens of *Catch-22*. Note the self-interest present in Dobbs, but unquestionably the ending of the chapter brings with it an increase in tension. Is Orr dead – or has he survived?

Mae West A life-jacket, named after the 'sex-symbol' film star.

'What's good for M & M enterprises is good for the country' The reversal is the truth, but here again is satire against big business.

trolling Singing.

Dixie-cup A disposable paper cup, used for ice-cream, beverages etc.

demurring Objecting.

mucid sibilance Probably a kind of hissing sound.

polychromatic Many-coloured.

Orr was an eccentric midget . . . The irony of all this is that Yossarian is quite wrong – Orr is working things out in his own way. He 'wins' by 'losing', like the old man in Rome.

andirons Firedogs for supporting wood on hearth.

cheesecake i.e. picture magazines containing scantily dressed girls.

cranberry-red elation Again one of the sudden images of nature that run throughout *Catch-22*.

Chapter 29, Peckem

No news of Orr is received – and in addition there is no parade. Scheisskopf is now a Colonel on Peckem's staff; there is a critical appraisal of Peckem's style and of Scheisskopf's dimness and obsession with parades. The feud between Peckem and Dreedle means that Peckem is out to capture Dreedle's bomb groups. At once, there is jealousy between Cargill and Scheisskopf. The bombing of a village is discussed, with humanists like Dunbar and Yossarian in opposition to Korn; but the latter blackmails them by threatening to send them on dangerous missions instead of this particular 'milk-run'. Cathcart undertakes the final briefing, alternately confident and abject, dedicating the mission (which should produce a fine aerial photograph of neat bombing) to General Peckem.

tickler file A memorandum pad, a memory-aid.
effulgent Radiant.
augmenting . . . oral This should be read with great attention – it shows Peckem's culture and his use of it; he avoids the usual manner of expression by his own literary style – which is affected, flamboyant.
Plato (427–347 BC) The great philosopher, born in Athens of noble birth.
Nietzsche (1844–1900) The philosopher who propounded the theory that strength is admirable, and weakness a vice.
Montaigne (1533–1592) Moralist, thinker and essayist.
Theodore Roosevelt (1858–1919) Twenty-sixth President of the United States, also a noted sportsman and explorer.
the Marquis de Sade (1740–1814) Author of a number of licentious romances, died mad; the word 'sadistic' comes from his name.
Warren G. Harding (1865–1923) President of the United States in 1921, where he promoted the Washington Peace Conference.
apothegms Terse pointed sayings.
bons mots Effective witty sayings.
Fortinbras . . . *Hamlet* Fortinbras is the Prince of Norway. In the final scene he acknowledges the nobility of the dead Hamlet.
Pentagon Headquarters of the United States defence forces.

Chapter 30, Dunbar

Dunbar deliberately drops his bombs beyond the village. Yossarian gets McWatt back as pilot, and still reverts from time to time to the death of Snowden. McWatt performs many aerial tricks, the most frightening being his buzzing the beach. One of these ends in disaster, with Kid Sampson being sliced in half.

Daneeka is supposed to be in the plane but isn't, and McWatt flies into a mountain. The pressures on the men are very much in evidence.

One of the most dramatic and searing chapters in the novel. Dunbar demonstrates his humanity, or perhaps the war has 'scrambled his brains'. McWatt certainly can't resist his current tendencies; having murdered, he commits suicide. The laconic last sentence of the chapter (the raising of the number of missions yet again) intimates that perhaps it is best for men to die naturally in war.

pilgrimage ... shrine Imagery appropriate to the Chaplain's position.
buzz your tent i.e. fly low over it.
callipygous ass i.e. having shapely buttocks.
bangs Fringes (of hair).
like pet puppy dogs against the shore Note the innocence of this image, which contrasts so vividly with the terrible event that is to come.
Kid Sampson had rained all over This is grotesque but terrible. The same thing happened to Yossarian with Snowden and it shows that everyone is involved in war. Kid Sampson's leap in part reflects the pressure and stress the men are under.
Colonel Cathcart was so upset There is a black irony about this: if two men die the others have to be brought correspondingly nearer death.

Revision questions on Chapters 21–30

1 Give an account of the scene in which Yossarian appears nude, indicating what you find amusing about it.

2 Say in what ways the profit motive is important in these chapters.

3 Compare and contrast either the Chaplain and Corporal Whitcomb *or* Cathcart and Korn *or* Nately and Aarfy.

4 Write an account of the part played by either Orr or Major Sanderson or Dunbar.

5 Write an account of the exchanges between Peckem and Scheisskopf.

Chapter 31, Mrs Daneeka

This short chapter is a merciless send-up of military 'bull' – of hidebound attitudes and actions. Daneeka – thought to be in

McWatt's plane although he manifestly isn't – is reported dead, his widow deriving great material benefits. The Whitcomb–Cathcart condolence form is therefore sent out in all its grotesque and ridiculous regulation nullity. Having been declared dead, Daneeka can do nothing about it. The ironies of the situation are compounded, with Mrs Daneeka not only acquiring wealth but also male friends. Even in this kind of novel Heller manages to convey the pathos of Daneeka's isolation.

a fraternal lodge i.e. Daneeka was a freemason. But read on to see what benefits Mrs Daneeka derives – Heller's account is a satire on the American way of death.
pullulating Sprouting, developing, breeding.
PX rations Supplied by the Post Exchange, equivalent to our NAAFI.
Words cannot express the deep personal grief Satirical, of letters of condolence in general, but condemning outright the blatant hypocrisy of this one.

Chapter 32, Yo-Yo's Roomies

Yossarian is thinking of Kid Sampson's legs washed up on the beach. A group of all-American patriotic boys move in with Yossarian, who is very upset by this. Chief White Halfoat gives some impetus to the joke about Doc Daneeka; Captain Black bullies the new fliers, and the latter get rid of the 'dead man' in Yossarian's tent.

Yossarian, with Kid Sampson and Snowden running through his mind, thinks constantly of death. Again the reversal technique is employed, or the high spirits of the new arrivals should cheer but only depress. Yossarian's flight to Rome is from them as much as death.

They were horsing around ... They had listened to the World Series They were ragging one another and playing about ... They had listened on radio to the major baseball competition in the States. This paragraph satirizes the unthinking, innocent, naïve patriotic approach of these young airmen who are about to see combat.
Donald Duck's nephews The legendary cartoon character created by Walt Disney. There is a cartoon element in the presentation of these young men
rambunctious Wild, unruly.

Chapter 33, Nately's Whore

Yossarian in Rome, where 'big shots' are holding Nately's girl captive. Dunbar, Dobbs and Hungry Joe rescue her from these naked men, and it even becomes something of a tactical farce, particularly from the point of view of the senior officers. Nately goes to bed with his girl, and then sees her go out street-walking.

Promiscuity and sex are the themes of this chapter, as indeed of all the Rome sequences. Nately's innocence is alternately endearing or maddening.

a wizard at directing a pincer movement This section is laced with clichés – the officers talk in terms of tactics, almost as if they cannot escape from the current military jargon they use.
Smith . . . Radcliffe . . . Bryn Mawr Women's colleges of high academic and social status in the United States.
'Che succede?' What's going on?
'pazzo' Crazy (slang).
'Madonn'!' Madonna. (Here an exasperated, semi-humorous appeal to the 'Mother of God'.)
'Va fongul' Clear off (obscene).
'Lasciami!' Leave me alone.
transmogrified i.e. transformed in a magical or surprising manner.
Congress . . . The House of Representatives In the United States system of government, Congress consists of the Senate, elected by the state legislatures, and the House of Representatives, elected directly by the people.

Chapter 34, Thanksgiving

The Thanksgiving day sick joke, which upsets Yossarian so much that he knocks Nately out. Both Yossarian and Dunbar thought that Milo was attacking the squadron again. They visit Nately in hospital and find the Chaplain there also with a case of 'Wisconsin shingles'. Then a soldier in white is brought into the ward and a hysterical outburst follows, with Dunbar asserting that there is no one inside the bandages. Nurse Duckett reveals to Yossarian that 'they are going to disappear' Dunbar – another menacing twist. It is obviously felt that he has gone mad.

The frenetic action is followed by a kind of hospital gathering which reflects the chapter title rather more accurately than the day itself.

saturnalia Ancient Roman festival, now applied to scene of wild revelry.

It was indeed, the same man There is an element of sickness in this because it is the same man only in the sense that it is any wounded-beyond-saving soldier, the unknown soldier recognized by Yossarian earlier.

'It isn't even good grammar' Yossarian has his own cynical wit at times.

Chapter 35, Milo the Militant

Nately insists on flying more missions. Milo plunders his country-men, and consequently is very highly thought of. He goes to Cathcart and asks to fly more missions; then demonstrates that he is indispensable to everybody, and that business cannot be run without him. Naturally, he does not have to fly the missions. A bargain is struck whereby all the men in the squadron have to fly Milo's missions since he is doing so much for them. Dobbs and Nately are both killed in the next raid.

This is a study in manipulation. The man who is indispensable survives, the profit motive rules again, as always. Nately is on a course for death anyway because of his obsessive wish to be with his girl, Chief White Halcoat dies almost unnoticed (the war is taking its toll either directly or obliquely). Milo is a student of social psychology of the kind that ensures he gets what he wants by putting the ideas into impressionable minds.

Cape Cod. C.O.D. Note the pun – but the letters of course stand for Cash on Delivery.

peas . . . high seas From now on the comedy is heightened by the repetition and the rhyming sequence and the ritual – almost like the 'This is the house that Jack Built' – a pyramid of increasing commodities. Interested students will unravel the rest of this paragraph – suffice it to say that Milo is 'blinding' Cathcart with his range of reference.

Piltdown man A reference to the ('planted') skull found in 1913 and until 1953 believed to belong to prehistoric man. (A famous archaeological hoax.)

'We have coals in Newcastle, sir' A reference to the proverb: the ridiculousness of taking things to a place which already has plenty of them – not that this would be a deterrent to Milo.

For once, a military intelligence report proved accurate An ironic aside, stressing that most of these reports were notoriously inaccurate.

zigged when he should have zagged Ridiculous phrase, perhaps indicating the lottery of survival.

like a water-lily on the dark-blue sea A fine poetic image contrasting with the violence of the action.

Chapter 36, The Cellar

The chaplain broods about the twelve men killed in the action. But just as he becomes aware of the atmosphere overhanging the field he is himself taken away and interrogated about the signatures of the mail – with of course Whitcomb and Cathcart on the interrogators' side. He is released with threats. On his way back he meets Colonel Korn, and taxes him with the fact that the men have flown seventy missions, with the loss of twelve men that day. Korn points out to him that Peckem is now in charge, not Dreedle (whom the Chaplain claims to know).

The sickness of death is seen in the gloating of Whitcomb (death, so to speak, gives him a job and thus a reason for living). There is a further emphasis on the isolation and ineffectuality of the chaplain. No spiritual or moral reason can deflect the course of man's injustice to man.

'Sure he's guilty . . . guilty as hell' Note the interrogation techniques, with assumptions and prejudices – and look back at the interrogation of Clevinger along the same lines. This is another example of 'the enemy within', and in a sense Clevinger and the chaplain are both outsiders.
'Leave the drip . . . that doesn't bother me' Note the irony – the interrogator is leaving it for himself *not* for the victim; in other words, there is no humanity or compassion for one of his kind.
Q.E.D. *Quod erat demonstrandum* – 'which was the thing to be proved'.
Colonel Cathcart stepped into the basement as though from a closet There is a kind of humour in this – a parody of interrogation techniques.
hot tomato See note p.37.
notarized affidavit A witnessed, sworn statement.
the jig's up i.e. the game's up, you're found out.

Chapter 37, General Scheisskopf

The shortest chapter in the whole novel – and in a sense the most grotesque. The surprising (or is it?) promotion of Scheisskopf to General, now ranking above Peckem. The army moves in a mysterious way its blunders to perform.

Chapter 38, Kid Sister

Yossarian refusing to fly any more missions – goes to see the dead Nately's girl, and is viciously attacked by her. (Much of the grotesque element of the novel emerges in the ingenuity with which she times and plans further attacks – completely impossible and unrealistic –

on Yossarian.) Yossarian's revolt brings him single friends at night, like Appleby, and we learn that Major Major has disappeared. Captain Black comes with the news that everyone has been cleared out of Rome – including, of course, Nately's whore's kid sister.

Achilles The most famous of the Greek heroes at the siege of Troy, invulnerable except in one heel.

she sat with her tempestuous, proud, lovely head bowed Note the elevated language (the rhyme above gives a kind of poetry). In view of her occupation and nature, it is of course ironic.

leery Wary.

Atabrine tablets See note p.30.

a real royal screwing i.e. putting more pressure on. Paradoxical use of term, which usually means particularly pleasurable sexual intercourse.

that kid Nately's body spinning in his grave Further evidence of the sadistic nature of Captain Black, who always enjoyed teasing Nately about his whore.

Chapter 39, The Eternal City

In the opinion of this reader, the outstanding chapter of the novel. It owes much to the surrealistic elements, particularly in the grotesque, inhuman, nightmare deviations from acceptable living that are the features of Yossarian's walk. The chapter is symbolic, almost a *Pilgrim's Progress* through war and through life; consequently, it should be read with a keen eye for the way in which Heller creates the mordant atmosphere that is its main characteristic. Life is funny, but here the whiplash of Heller's humour is stilled; and instead he exposes, in a series of strongly visual incidents, the terrifying and depraved instances of man's intolerable abuse of man.

At the beginning of the chapter Milo is trying to get Yossarian to conform and to stop rocking the boat, as he puts it. Rome is now in ruins; Yossarian goes searching for the kid sister, but learns that all the girls have been chased away by the military police. The old woman who informs him of this says it is because of Catch-22. Milo helps him to search for the girl; but Yossarian walks through the streets and registers the disgusting sights in his already sickened consciousness. Each incident reveals the sick nature of man, man who has forgotten kindness and compassion. There is an equally terrible description too of Aarfy's killing of the maid by throwing her out of the window – this is part of the nightmare. Then Yossarian is arrested for being in Rome without a pass, and taken back to Korn and Cathcart, who tell him that they are going to send him home.

The Colosseum The amphitheatre in Rome, built about AD 72, which staged gladiatorial combats and saw the death of many Christian martyrs.

carabinieri Soldiers.

All the poor young girls were gone An echo of the song 'Where are all the flowers gone?'

Catch-22 did not exist, he was positive of that But it does, and though Yossarian rebels he cannot get around it, except by desertion.

Illegal tobacco Milo's human sympathies are quickly stilled at the thought of doing a deal or making money.

The tops of the sheer buildings slanted . . . the street seemed tilted The effect is cinematic – almost like a Batman film – but it is strongly visual, projected from the imagination: a superb synthesis of Yossarian's mood and his surroundings.

catatonic eyes Eyes with a fixed, trance-like expression.

How many cockroaches and landlords would triumph? A series of rhetorical questions show that there are no answers, that the misery and suffering of humanity is such that no individual can measure it. Echoes educational session – ask the unanswerable.

how Christ must have felt as he walked through the world A moving, human analogy, a reflection on sin, suffering, degradation and deviation.

walking on human teeth The surrealist effect, almost of a painting, is very vivid here.

a slew A great number, large amount (US colloquialism).

Then he threw her out of the window Perhaps an indication of Aarfy's state of mind, the sickness that war generates and which is reflected in all that Yossarian has seen.

They arrested Yossarian . . . They apologized to Aarfy Again, the wonderful capacity of the military to blunder, to arrest on a technicality rather than for murder. But there is more to it than this, for Yossarian is wanted by Cathcart and Korn, as we discover.

Chapter 40, Catch-22

The deal with Cathcart and Korn is that Yossarian is to be sent home (he is disturbing morale on the base), promoted and given another medal – in return for which he will join Cathcart and Korn, become pals with them, and give good reports of them when he gets home. He accepts the deal – or appears to.

Another stress on manipulation for personal ends. Falsification is the order of the day, but the disturbed nature of Yossarian's mind is shown with the reappearance of Nately's whore.

oak leaf clusters i.e. additional awards.

'sprit de corps Loyalty.

Like us. Join us . . . Say nice things about us here and back in the States A piece of consummate blackmail—join the establishment, conform, do as you're told, and you'll be all right—we'll send you home. Perhaps the classic way of dealing with free expression. Certainly the chapter ends with an 'old pals act'.

Chapter 41, Snowden

Yossarian in hospital after the assault upon him. He is anaesthetized, and wakes up from time to time; in one of his lucid moments he confides in the chaplain about his deal with Cathcart and Korn. The chaplain tells him of the death of Hungry Joe in his sleep, with the cat on his face. On one occasion, Yossarian wakes, feeling cold, and reverts as ever to the cold that Snowden felt as he lay dying. That terrible time after Avignon is now told with a realism that makes a poignant, moving, stomach-wrenching contrast with the tone of so much of the book. Yet we have been prepared for it all the time – and the passage reveals, just as the chapter on 'The Eternal City' revealed, Heller's abiding humanity, and his concern for suffering and the loneliness of those who suffer. There are times when one feels that *Catch-22* has been in part misread as a novel – that its seriousness of purpose and commitment have been overlooked in the firework display of its wit and raillery and innuendo.

Which one is the scalpel? Further satire on the medical profession.

finky Slang for something more obscene.

The only ones left are me A moment of terrible pathos which largely accounts for Yossarian's mental state. All his friends are dead.

The raw muscles inside twitched like live hamburger meat An image redolent of the realism Heller is trying to convey. He succeeds because of the startling quality of the image and the fact he is describing like and like.

found only Milo's note and a bottle of aspirin Perhaps the last of the cynical appraisals of profit at the expense of life—but a telling one.

Snowden's insides slithered down to the floor You will see 'stomach-wrenching' in the account above. This is the most realistic and terrible moment of the novel, for this *is* the finality of death; the words towards the end of this chapter say it all and underline what I have said about Heller's compassion (pp.463–4).

Chapter 42, Yossarian

Yossarian tells Danby that he is going to reject the deal with Colonel

Korn, but Danby tells him about the other report which is being put about that he has been involved in black market activities. He even learns that Aarfy is prepared to turn witness against him. As Yossarian observes to Danby, 'When I look up ... I see people cashing in on every decent impulse and every human tragedy.' He says that now he will think of himself; and just afterwards the chaplain bursts in with the great news that Orr has got himself into Sweden. Yossarian realizes at last what Orr was trying to say to him, and decides, much to the chaplain's approval, that he too will desert. Danby presses money on him, and he leaves.

The widespread and effective nature of blackmail to obtain conformity is central to this final chapter, and the high-sounding phrases, as ever, are the hypocritical cover for reality. The rejection of war, the preservation of sanity, the few refusing to accept the wishes and then the dictatorship of the many are symbolized at the end – the open end – of the novel. If you have integrity, moral courage, to go against the tide, you may survive.

exophthalmic Having protruding eyeballs.

Ideals are good ... you must try to look up at the big picture Danby's idealism is rejected by Yossarian, who has a clear idea of what human nature is like.

Revision questions on Chapters 31–42

1 What do you consider to be the most horrifying incident in these chapters? Give reasons for your answer.

2 Indicate the part played by the old man in these chapters.

3 Give an account of the effect of the continual raising of the number of missions on any three of the characters, including Yossarian.

4 Write an essay on Heller's creation of atmosphere in the chapter called 'The Eternal City'.

5 Write an account of Snowden's death. How far do you think it accounts for Yossarian's reactions throughout the novel?

Character and caricature

After reading most novels one can generally write character sketches of some if not all of the characters met with in the fictional experience. In *Catch-22* this is not the case, for Joseph Heller has deliberately chosen to make his 'characters' idiosyncratic; an amalgam of traits, obsessions, neuroses, manners of speaking; registering the types of human reaction of men under the stress of wartime conditions, when the physical and emotional demands made on them are sometimes too great for them to accept.

Yossarian

Unquestionably, the hero is Yossarian, yet how much do we know of him? The answer is that we know his reactions to his current situation, we know that one experience (and others) has so eaten itself into his consciousness that it reappears as a 'daymare', the focus of his brooding, of his fears and of the essence of his revolt. The pressures on Yossarian are great, for he loses all his friends, with the exception of Orr; and feels that there is something wrong with the human condition, that it can so wilfully destroy itself. His sensitivity is never in question – he not only broods on Snowden but on the killing of Kraft as well, and his flippancy, wit and ability to joke are all reflexes against the intolerable stress of too many missions. I suppose it could be argued that his excessive sexual energy is a reflex too, and one feels the disoriented nature of his life – away from combat when you should try to cram into your life all the things you need to make you sane, but at the same time be mature enough to deal with them in your stride. But Yossarian, who fakes illness, *is* ill: sick of the war; sick of the fearful experiences of it; of Snowden; of Kid Sampson; of the driving ruthlessness of Korn. He almost does a deal, but fortunately his experiences away from the battle prove to be vital in his rejection of it. The real insight into Yossarian's consciousness comes when he walks through the Eternal City, as the eternal pilgrim passing through life and seeing with a frightful intensity the nature of depraved and degraded man. In a sense, hospital is Yossarian's spiritual retreat; his jokes the reactions of a man scared of the repetition of terrible events – individual deaths that cannot be erased from the memory or, especially, the heart.

Yossarian is not a rounded character in any sense of the term: yes, we live through that nightmare walk; the scene on the beach when Kid Sampson is sliced in two; the other scene when Yossarian watches those symbolic mushrooms reach up through the land; and the terror and vomiting when Snowden's frightful message is spilled out over him. We understand his choice: his recognition of Orr's message just before it is too late; his humanitarian values; his outsider-Assyrian stance; his fears that Milo is again bombing the squadron, and his assault on Nately as a result. But of Yossarian *not* in reflex and reaction we see virtually nothing – his way of life is unknown to us, for he is presented as a man at a particular time and place. He has no past, and characters in fiction achieve psychological integration because of what they were as well as what they are. He is a rebel, a fraud, a joker, a frightened man; he is over-sexed, humane, twisted, sardonic, kind. In short, he is the paradox of humanity, with an infinite capacity for both lying and telling the truth. In a settled and ordered way of life he would stand out; in a situation that is at once apocalyptic and claustrophobic, he responds as the type of sufferer that cannot win. His is the tragedy of sensitivity, a character trait for which there is no cure!

The chaplain

The chaplain is, in a sense, much more human and rounded: he has a past, a wife whom he loves and cherishes, and he recurs to the beautiful things in that past, like their love-making and their mutual understanding. But he shares with Yossarian one quality: he is an outsider, shy, withdrawn; living on the periphery of pseudo-civilization in the woods with the unsympathetic Corporal Whitcomb (later Sergeant) – who spends some time checking up on him and certainly scores over him by having the letter of condolence adopted as standard issue. He tries hard to stand up for the men, but though he complains on their account he is put down with relative ease by the hypocrisy of Cathcart and the uncompromising assertiveness of Korn. Humiliated by both, he goes to the officers' club when his star is in the ascendant, and withdraws from it when it isn't.

The chaplain's pursuit of Major Major is, like everyone else's, unsuccessful; he is uncertain, has a vivid imagination that drives him to the outer limits of apprehension when he thinks his wife may be disloyal, his children raped or murdered. But he has one salient quality – he is loyal, loyal to the point of almost becoming articulate. His pathetic attempts to do the right thing – going to see the men in the ward – are more than compensated for by his sheer delight (he is not of the establishment in spirit or in being) in the fact that Orr has escaped to Sweden. His vision of the naked man in the tree, and his interpretation of it, is as real as the *déjà vu* experiences that worry him so much. Like Major Danby, the chaplain endears himself to us, because he too might be taken outside to be shot – after all he has only qualities of common humanity on his side – not power. He develops throughout the novel: he decides to stay and fight on.

Orr

Orr registers very strongly with the reader: he is practical, down-to-earth, but with a certain low cunning that Yossarian fails to interpret. He is always making crash-landings, but just as the repairs to the stove must be right, so the landings are the rehearsals for the ultimate in crash landings – the one that leads to escape. Curiously, Yossarian finds Orr defenceless, a 'midget', a 'gnome'. But Yossarian fears a bad pilot; and is superstitious enough to think that Orr's flying with the squadron is enough to get everybody into trouble. Orr's 'war nerves' can be seen in his giggling reactions; in his doing practical things to keep himself occupied; and in his 'joke' – which was really serious, a kind of death wish – of getting himself hit over the head.

Havermeyer

All the characters of *Catch-22* are caricatures in the sense that each reflects the pressures of combat – their differences are seen by the different ways in which they escape them – drink, sex, violence, escapades, so that even with Havermeyer one can feel some sympathy. He is the best bombardier, the one who takes unnecessary risks, the kind that can get others into trouble; his relaxation is shooting mice with home-made dumdum bullets, but we have to remember that this is a success situation for him: his escape from it is to keep himself in constant training for the next round. To see Havermeyer simply as a sadist – and he is one – is to see him too simply; he is one of the combat men reacting in his own way to the pressures; and being the best is his reward – being seen to be the best is a kind of decoration he is complacent enough to wear permanently.

Clevinger

Clevinger, like Yossarian, is the natural outsider, the intellectual who has done nothing and therefore is fair game for the representatives of the establishment – for thinkers are dangerous and must therefore be reduced. The early scene of his interrogation, with Scheisskopf defending and prosecuting him, is a frightful example of the military way of measurement by contradiction; of the denial of any kind of expression; of the repression of anything that smacks of individuality.

McWatt

McWatt has, basically, the same kind of reactions as Havermeyer – a delight in danger, which, on one terrible occasion, goes too far and spreads Kid Sampson over those on the beach. Yossarian is always cursing him ineffectually when he is in action, but McWatt's own pressures, and the clear knowledge of what he has done, make him take the other way out: suicide.

Dunbar

Dunbar is another who suffers greatly. Like Yossarian, he kids along in the ward, joins in the trips to Rome, makes his unavailing dive for Nurse Duckett; but then the bombing of the village eats into his soul, and he begins to waste away. He is further undermined by 'the reappearance' of the plaster-and-bandage-encased soldier; and after the argument on the ward – or, rather, the hysteria that is generated – we are told that he will be 'disappeared'. Dunbar, like many of the combat pilots we meet, cannot stand the loss of humanity involved in war.

Hungry Joe

Hungry Joe and Chief White Halfoat are much more on the caricature level, though both predict their own deaths. Hungry Joe is on the voyeuristic level as well: his impotent camera is inevitably at the ready, clicking at each salacious detail. His neurosis is a need for perpetual motion even when asleep, for his active mind continues to overspill and his nightmares are the talk of the camp. Huple's cat, we remember, constantly sleeps on his face and ultimately kills him.

Chief White Halfoat

He is the assistant intelligence officer, and lives positively in the past, with his myth (?) of the oil findings; he and his tribe have been moved on constantly; and he is a heavy drinker, constantly siphoning off supplies.

Captain Flume

He is so scared by Chief White Halfoat that he takes to the woods, while still preparing his publicity releases. Flume, too, is a neurotic, but only emerges periodically – to scare (in his turn) the chaplain.

Doc Daneeka

A caricature of the on-the-make doctor who is himself a hypo-chondriac; he tries to evade service by rigging his own medical, for he does not wish to leave his lucrative practice with its overtones of corruption. He has his own brand of sick humour, but opts out of everything as far as he can; he defines the expression 'catch-22', and is himself truly caught in it when he is thought to be in the plane crashed by McWatt. From then on he is 'dead', and his pathetic letters to his wife are of no avail: the military pronouncement is final; and the black comedy is carried to its ludicrous conclusion with the men not speaking to Doc-who-is-no-longer-there. Perhaps we remember one human action, though, when we think back: Doc is there when the mission to Avignon returns and tenderly wraps Yossarian in a blanket as he emerges with liquid Snowden all over him.

Peckem and Dreedle

The caricature element is best seen in the delineation of the top brass and their minions. There is an element too of music-hall comedy about their names: the Laurel and Hardy associations of Peckem and Dreedle, Cathcart and Korn, are obvious. But the appalling thing is that these are men of power; *Peckem* is a pedantic literary incompetent, *Dreedle* an ignoramus who flaunts his closeness to his attractive nurse, emasculates his son-in-law, and thinks that he has the power to shoot men out of hand. It is not only the incompetence of these two men that is pilloried here, but also the fact that they are in competition with each other; that they are a mass of contradictions; and that, in Peckem's case, he is superseded by a person whose limitations have been made apparent to all except those who rule.

Cathcart and Korn

These two are rather different in calibre from Peckem and Dreedle. *Cathcart* is slightly more than a caricature, since he is examined in some depth. He has a superiority complex and at the same time an inferiority complex: he is self-confident and abject; bullying and cringing; abrasive and hypocritical; his own best friend, his own worst enemy. He rejects the chaplain when he himself has done something wrong that might show; but tolerates him when he thinks he can use him. We understand Dobbs's wish to kill him, for Cathcart's function in the novel is to drive men to the edge of insanity – and beyond – by continually raising the number of missions they have to fly. He is ruled by an overweening ambition and is a snob with a power complex, totally without a sense of perspective. Thus, when McWatt crashes and Kid Sampson is killed he raises the number of missions, as a reflex to losing two men. When Yossarian goes over the target twice and costs Kraft his life, Cathcart awards him a medal. His impetuous decisions hang by a flimsy thread of mood or temper, reaction or despair.

But if Cathcart comes across as an unsympathetic character, *Korn* is malign: he rules by coldness, appreciates his position as the power behind Cathcart (they exist in a state of mutual hatred). Korn makes decisions for Cathcart that the latter is then too weak to resist; and delights in humiliating anyone he comes in contact with – particularly the chaplain. He is behind the

projected deal with Yossarian; and his only bad moment comes
when, after his inspired briefing of the men, he learns that
General Dreedle has become sick of him.

Scheisskopf

Like Peckem and Dreedle, he too is an enemy within: a man
obsessed by his need for petty achievement; a little boy playing
with toy soldiers who happen to be men. His first major triumph
is of course the swingless marching; and it is obvious from the
tone of the novel that this is but a foretaste of things to come:
things that are generally covered by such words as 'unimagina-
tive', 'dull', 'mechanical', mediocre'. The promotion of Scheisskopf to General illustrates one of the main theses of the book:
the bigot of limited ability is the man most likely to succeed in
the armed forces.

Minor characters

Each of these is memorable only in terms of a particular salient
quality. For instance, the over-sexed nature of *Scheisskopf's wife*
and her appallingly conventional non-belief in a good God; *Whitcomb's* mean and belittling rejection of the chaplain, and his
literary architecture on the condolence letter; *Kid Sampson's*
singing and impetuous leaping-up at McWatt's 'buzz'. *Piltchard
and Wren* provide further comedy cross-talk, though merely
echoing each other – for they have never had it so good as in the
war. They are offset by the ineffectuality of *Danby*, but Danby
has the saving grace of appreciating Yossarian and holding to
decent standards of behaviour and reason in his relationships.
Towser, Knight, Luciana and *Nately's whore* are all seen briefly and
tellingly – the last two perhaps in frenetic parody action of what
Italian girls are *supposed* to be like: fiery, temperamental, aggressive, tempestuous and unpredictable.

There are other eccentrics who balance one another within
the framework of the action, like *Major Major* and *Major—de
Coverley*; the first is treated in some depth psychologically,
though it could be argued that his father has as much space in
the narrative as he does. Marked forever by the double name
and the resemblance to Henry Fonda, wanting not rank but

friendship, Major Major withdraws from all contact: essentially shy, he engages in the criminal activity of altering memoranda (Peckem's word) by signing variations of Washington Irving and John Milton. Major—de Coverley pitching horseshoes, entering Rome to be flower scarred, saying 'Gimme eat' in refutation of Captain Black's loyalty oath – and doing an egg deal with Milo – all this adds up to a larger-than-life cartoon figure, rightly an enigma to both sides, his own and the enemy. He seems to belong to an earlier war.

Aarfy, Black and *Nately* are placed together here because they form a spectrum of morality: *Aarfy* is deaf to Yossarian, apparently conventional in his pipe-smoking complacency, but his killing of the maid and the throwing of the body out of the window is a moment of horror – perhaps he too has cracked under the strain of the missions and this is his terrible way of expressing it. It is, however, possible that he is an example of total insensibility, for he threatens to throw the girl out of the window well before he does so. There is grand irony when Yossarian is arrested and he is not.

Black is the reverse, a sadist who enjoys the thought of the men being terrified of having to fly over Bologna, perpetuates the joke about the new invention which will glue planes together in the air, and enjoys needling Nately by constantly sleeping with his whore. *Nately* himself represents decency – of upbringing, of behaviour, of kindness and consideration: he is the eternal 'sucker' who tries to do good and usually suffers as a result. He tries to stop Yossarian when he rampages through the camp, and ends up in hospital after Yossarian has knocked him down: even then he is embarrassed and ashamed at being the focus of attention. He is romantic and chivalrous, thinking how nice it would be if his friends married the girls they sleep with in Rome. For a long time he is too 'decent' to sleep with his own girl. He inspires in Yossarian the desire to return to Rome in search of the kid sister.

I have saved until last in this section those two astute businessmen who operate their own version of Catch-22, and who ensure that they will never be caught. *Milo* is a masterpiece, 'M & M Enterprises' dominating the action of the book; he is not so much a character, more a way of consummate crookedness, which is not likely to be brought down. His most audacious gamble, the anti-Red-Cross action of bombing his own squadron, and his subsequent explanation (which is accepted by the great wise public at large), ensures the continuing success of his operations. Milo demonstrates by his career that you can fool all the public all the time if you can make money – and also if you can lose it. Money, not strategy, runs the war. He is the profound example of the superficial: being sympathetic, friendly, patronizing, ingratiating – then taking off for his next venture. Milo's reception in Palermo; the offices he comes to hold; his return to Rome ('Marchese Milo'): all these demonstrate his power; the unscrupulous nature of his business; the worship of money by the gullible; the fact that buying and selling, not fighting and killing, determine the quality of life.

Milo offers to fly more missions, and then shows that he cannot be spared to do so, unless Cathcart (woefully inadequate) can control his business. He is the great manipulator, the conman of the military, and his merger with *Wintergreen* is hardly surprising, since Wintergreen himself has, in his time, manoeuvred and virtually controlled the generals. The satire is clear: ideals cannot compete with trading, morality with money, military power with profit. These two characters will survive, for money buys immunity from the risks attendant upon those who do the actual fighting.

Structure, style and humour

The structure of *Catch-22* is circular, almost as if the trap of the title is being closed by the teeth of the words; we move about in time as in a dream or nightmare, always returning to the trap of the war or, in the case of Yossarian, to the trap of the consciousness, the memory of Snowden's death. The chronological sequence (which in most novels consists of straightforward narrative with occasional recurrences to the past), is dispensed with in *Catch-22* because war is the major disturbance of most people's chronology, and time is related to incidents, memories, tragedies, which come in irrational order anyway. Heller has used one technique, the stream of consciousness, the interior monologue, to great effect in the case of Yossarian and the chaplain. The latter's is simple – the memories of his marriage, the love of his wife, the brooding on the present and his incapacity to make friends and influence people – but Yossarian's is more complex. In his case, the past in America is never revealed; the past that is revealed is the past of death: the death of others in combat and accident.

The most important aspect of Heller's style in *Catch-22* is the use of repetition at all levels: the repeated event in the memory that is as immediate as when it took place; the repetition of words and conversations (Snowden's 'I'm cold'). Repetition is also the most important aspect of the structure, for everything is repeated: the bombing missions; the nightmares of Hungry Joe; the trips to Rome; the raising of the number of missions; the parades; the coming and going in hospital; the sexual indulgence. The effect is to encapsulate time, so that we spin on a wheel of associations, impressions, situations and facts.

The *déjà vu* of the chaplain is central to the structure of the novel, for we have been in most of the experiences and situations before; we have been told *something* of them before. The outstanding instance is, of course, the death of Snowden; and the structural technique is to give us more and more of the story in fragments until we build up to the final full story in Chapter 41, which is to give us the final full tragedy of war. The structure is consummate art – all the pieces fit the puzzle, all the spokes fit the wheel.

Here is work for the interested student; for it is possible to calculate the actual time sequence of the novel from the evidence of Yossarian's mind, and other related references. But the shape of the novel is probably designed by the author to show the disruptive and degrading effects of war by 'scrambling' the narrative. There is a cunning obliqueness about the structure: the chapter headings frequently do *not* deal with the person they name so much as with other people – almost as if the sense of perspective is deliberately destroyed. Again the immediate application is obvious: all those men who have to fly more and more combat missions have already had their perspectives destroyed. Notice, too, how there is almost frenetic movement from place to place as if movement were the one certain thing in an uncertain world. Mockery, exposure, realism: these are the pivotal points of *Catch-22*.

The details of Heller's methods are stimulating and various. As you will see from the textual notes, there is a continual use of paradox. Almost everything is a contradiction of accepted standards and judgements. Thus Black can say of Hitler that he 'had done such a great job of combating un-American activities in Germany' (p.42), while Colonel Cargill is described as 'a self-made man who owed his lack of success to nobody' (p.35). Another aspect of Heller's style is the use of parody again on various levels throughout the novel. The military manner of coercion through studied flattery is nowhere better exemplified than in Cargill's address to the squadron (pp.35–6).

Heller captures the authentic tone, the various manifestations of 'bull' that characterize any military establishment: the self-confident briefing of Korn; the barked responses of General Dreedle; Cathcart's bullying and hectoring; the ominous clichés of interrogation in the cases of Clevinger and the chaplain; and the literary pretentiousness of Peckem. Heller also has an eye and ear for the grotesque, firstly in comedy:

Orr giggled louder, infuriating her still further so that she flew up still higher into the air for another shot at his noodle, her wondrously full breasts soaring all over the place like billowing pennants in a strong wind . . . (p.32)

and secondly with a kind of serious surrealistic effect, as in Yossarian's walk through The Eternal City when he sees a young woman 'her whole face disfigured by a God-awful pink and piebald burn' (p.440). Previously he had found himself 'walking on human teeth lying on the drenched, glistening pavement near splotches of blood kept sticky by the pelting raindrops poking each one like sharp fingernails' (p.438). Here the effect reminds one of the more grotesque elements of Kafka's physical descriptions in the two novels I refer to in the textual notes. There are many grotesque incidents as well as descriptions in *Catch-22*; for example, Milo's bombing of the squadron; Havermeyer's light torture of the mice in his tent at night; and, perhaps best, the 're-appearance' of the soldier in white, elaborately described in his death-in-life immobility. Frequently the grotesque and the symbolic are linked; the terrible sights seen and heard by Yossarian in Rome on that nightmare walk are symbolic of the nature of life – licentiousness, brutality, contempt for the old by the young, abuse of the young by the old, instances of sickness (removal of teeth, convulsions) – all these are symbolic of a disintegration that follows the widespread disintegration of war. Obviously the tone is one of strong moral condemnation.

Another fine example of the use of symbol occurs when Yossarian, having turned back from Bologna, sees mushrooms growing, spawned by the rain (p.156). This is a nightmare, and the growth is the growth of death, the insistence of it, and Yossarian's fear that it is coming for him; the mushrooms are also the bodies of the dead, fungoid souls speaking to Yossarian of the unalterable destiny of man. Heller's fine use of symbol is matched by a proliferation of imagery which spans the novel in economical and sudden asides. Frequently the metaphor or simile is drawn from nature, almost as if that is the only permanent thing left in the world: even General Dreedle's nurse 'bloomed like a fertile oasis'; Yossarian watches the spread of blood 'like an enormous sea monster rising to devour him', Major—de Coverley has 'an angry shock of wild white hair' raging 'like a blizzard around his stern, patriarchal face'. There are many other images – from domestic and industrial life, for example – that show Heller's figurative flair. But while there are no deliberately flat areas of narrative, there is a careful use of cliché – the cliché that is really military jargon, the cliché of orders, the last refuge of dull minds stricken with apathy or impotence. And frequently these clichés are uttered unheard, for the satiric edge of Heller's style captures our favourite device of talking to others but listening only to ourselves. Does

Major—de Coverley listen to Milo? No; he says what Milo has said – just as Piltchard takes up where Wren has left off, because anyway he hasn't heard what Wren has said.

The ironic tone also informs the novel, and its targets are military intelligence, medical practice (or malpractice) and military obsession with triviality – and, as we have seen, a considered look at the eccentric and grotesque. Graphic narrative is also well in evidence, as when, for example, the attack on La Spezia is described, or even when McWatt swoops down on the beach. But there is one facet of Heller's style that deserves special mention, and that is the realism and the metaphorical realism of his writing. There is the realism of fact – Snowden's wounds, for example, but on occasions that realism is heightened by the use of figurative language: it strengthens rather than compares the facts. Reread the instance when Yossarian first discovers Snowden's wounds (p.460). If this makes one feel sick – as indeed it should – then what does the following do?

was that a tube of slimy bone he saw running deep inside the gory scarlet flow behind the twitching, startling fibers of weird muscle? – was dripping blood in several trickles, like snow melting on eaves, but viscous and red, already thickening as it dropped. (p.461)

Heller has broken the word-barrier, conveyed the actuality without sparing the reader; it is Yossarian we feel for, just as we would feel for ourselves in a like situation. The image is the message, for the mention of the snow is singularly appropriate – it is as cold as Snowden, as cold as his name. And it is this realism that gives *Catch-22* both unity and balance, for all the humour of the novel (and it is rich in sickness and in health of utterance, from the wit of Yossarian to the flower in Major—de Coverley's eye) is offset by the reality that is the foreground of the novel. We have seen that the laughter runs all the way, but is at times muted by the strain of events. At times the laughter is silenced by tragedy; and the farce of Hungry Joe, of Yossarian being attacked by Nately's whore, the sick farce of Milo doing all for the syndicate – all these are underpinned by the increasing number of missions, of deaths, of those who are 'disappeared'.

These are merely some indications of the nature of the structure, the style and the inherent humour of the novel. Look closely at the dialogue, at the cross-talk acts, at the antics, at the farcical situations, at those aspects of the novel discussed here, and see what they tell you of power, of human nature, of the truths of life. Style is the great clarifier of insinuation, but it is also the great cover too; for if we mock, ridicule and expose we reveal our feelings – but perhaps not our own replacement for what we hate. 'Yossarian jumped ... he took off' is the final statement of the novel. Such is Heller's craftsmanship that the image – of parachuting, of flying – is retained to the end. But the taking-off is into the unkown, not only for Yossarian, but for the reader too.

Satire

The Oxford English Dictionary defines satire as 'A poem, or in modern use sometimes a prose composition, in which prevailing vices or follies are held up to ridicule. This definition, further amplified, mentions the use of 'sarcasm, irony, ridicule', all of which are part of Joseph Heller's method in *Catch-22*. The keen edge of satire is, perhaps, first seen in English in the epigrammatic, antithetical verse of Dryden and Pope, where the influence of the classical form is apparent in the word order, the meticulous balance and the succinct delivery. Thus Dryden, writing of the Duke of Buckingham in his *Absalom and Achitophel* (1681), says that he was

A man so various that he seemed to be
Not one, but all mankind's epitome;
Stiff in opinions, always in the wrong,
Was everything by starts, and nothing long;

Now these lines ridicule, criticize, condemn, establishing a logical chain of progressive indictment; in the view of Dryden the person described is evil, and consequently the words are sharply chosen, pin-pricking character and personality traits. In Heller, on the other hand, the knife-cuts, in part, go beyond personality (though there are plenty of jabs at particular manifestations of human nature), to trace the broad areas of executive maladministration: the American services in wartime, and, behind the services, the immovable monolithic establishment. The real sweep of *Catch-22* takes in the top, then moves down, to expose all those areas affected by bureaucracy, inefficiency, misunderstanding, lack of common sense, profiteering, stupidity and the wilful and needless sacrifice of man to the demands of man. All these, and more, become apparent as one reads the novel; but do not be misled into thinking that *Catch-22* is merely a flippant categorizing of follies and vices. The morality behind *Catch-22* is an uncompromising one; among other things, it exposes 'the enemy within': general feuding with general; bombing attacks on one's own men; the debasing of the spiritual currency by licentiousness and self-indulgence, as escapes from the horrors of war.

The central definition of *Catch-22* is given on p.54. Yossarian realizes that he is 'caught', that they are all 'caught', so that *Catch-22*, the novel and the principle, is one long sick joke; just as war can be said to be a sick joke – and in order to get people to fight, and keep them fighting you have to provide a 'catch'. The satirical innuendo of *Catch-22* is, in part, against the conventional concept of patriotism and heroism – hence Yossarian's attitude towards the 'all-American' boys who come into his tent, and his life after Orr's disappearance. As early as Chapter 1 the first stabs are made straight into the flesh of the traditional concepts of decency, for 'The Texan turned out to be good-natured, generous and likeable. In three days no one could stand him'. Now the implication of this is that *not* to conform, i.e. not to be likeable but to be as you are, not someone else's man but your own, is laudable.

Throughout *Catch-22* we experience the topsy-turvy pattern of rejection, and probably the underlying irony is that war turns everything upside down anyway. The satire is strongly concerned with specific areas of hypocrisy, pettiness, success, and their concomitant evils. Milo Minderbinder is more important than the generals, because he buys and sells (often seemingly at a loss), but wherever he goes luxury and subservience attend him. There is no more incisive indication of this than when Milo, cunningly pleading that the men who fly the combat missions get all the glory and the medals, asks that he too may fly more missions. But this astute businessman has already planned for the answer, knowing that his own business details cannot be absorbed by appalled Colonel Cathcart, himself no mean black marketeer in plum tomatoes. Milo has shown that his business empire (nominally a giant 'co-operative' in which everyone has a share) is more important than the exigencies of war; and Heller underlines his achievements by tracing the upward curve of Milo's career, which contrasts with the downward curve of insanity and death of so many of Milo's comrades.

The satirical edge is felt keenly through character: the incompetence, ignorance and inhumanity of the generals and their mission-raising subordinates like Cathcart. The emphasis on military 'bull' runs thoughout the novel, with Scheisskopf highlighting the satire by his ridiculous attention to the details of parade competition – which is irrelevant to the war, but which leads to his promotion. Maladministration at all levels is apparent; even the important attack on Bologna turns out to be a 'milk run'. Military intelligence only proves right on one occasion, and then it is only factually correct about the towing out of the cruiser; it is signally silent about the flak that disposes of Dobbs and Nately.

The satire probes all aspects of military life on the station: the interrogation of Clevinger from spite, ignorance and protocol; the statistical existence of the dead man in Yossarian's tent, the sudden elevation of Major Major to Major Major Major; the awarding of a medal to Yossarian for an error. It extends far beyond this: the discovery of mysterious messages and intrigue in the simple name 'T. S. Eliot'; the arrest of Yossarian in Rome (but not of Aarfy, who has just thrown the maid's body out of the window); the interrogation of the chaplain in facile Hollywood-detective style. Then there is the incompetence and laziness of the doctors; the practice of a dubious psychiatry and – to return to Milo for a moment – the widespread nature of 'fiddling', of getting what you can out of the war. Perhaps the most poignant example of this is when Yossarian, opening the syrettes of morphine for the dying Snowden, finds a note which says 'What's good for M & M Enterprises is good for the country.'

There is satire on the good clean patriotic boys, on the need for games and relaxation, on men's sexual appetites in Rome, on the nature of the oversexed wife, on power, on perversion, on hyprocisy (see Cathcart), on ignorance, on names (consider the obvious obscene rhyme for Sue Ann Duckett). Students are recommended to search out for themselves the area of exposure in this novel, which seeks to define the futility of war, and of the power behind war – the financial interest that operates at the expense of moral and spiritual commitment (witness Yossarian and the chaplain). See also the section on 'Structure, style and humour', pp.70–74, for reference to the satirical tone and the nature of the humour implicit in *Catch-22*.

General questions

1 What aspects of military life are exposed in *Catch-22*? Refer closely to the text in your answer.

Guideline notes for essay answer

(a) Introduction – situation – Pianosa – state of war – aims – targets.

(b) Stretching men to utmost limits and beyond – deaths as a result and desertions – Kid Sampson, McWatt, Orr – neuresthenia and obsessions as a consequence of war – no adequate or competent medical supervision or examinations.

(c) Competition and jealousy among top brass and those in association with them – Dreedle, Peckem, Cathcart, Korn – stupid decisions – outward shows of discipline ridiculous – keep men occupied – skeet shooting – parades – corruption – mismanagement and incompetence – ambition – lack of integrity – building up of patriotism (the oath) – incidence of red tape/bureaucracy (censoring, names etc).

(d) Arbitrary promotions (Major Major) – appearance and reality (Major de—Coverley) – opportunism and abuse and the profit motive (Milo) – no spiritual importance (treatment of the chaplain) – arbitrary award of medals – incompetence of military police (Aarfy in Rome) – reversal of all human standards – need to be seen to be doing and to maintain prestige.

(e) Conclusion – incompetence at the top – lack of coordination – arbitrary orders – irrational decisions – intent on publicity – denial of humanity – motivated by fear and human complexes but not by truth or considered judgement.

2 Examine the roles played by Orr and Nately in the novel, saying clearly what you think each represents.
3 What elements of *Catch-22* do you find most horrifying and why? In your answer give evidence from the text.
4 Regarding Yossarian as a character, write an account of his main concerns and actions during the course of the novel.

5 Write an essay on the presentation of any *two* of the military hierarchy, from Cathcart and Korn upwards.

6 In what ways is *Catch-22* 'scrambled'? Refer closely to the text to support your views.

7 Write a detailed examination of any *one* chapter in the novel which seems to you to be of some importance to a complete understanding of its meaning.

8 In what ways is the chaplain inadequate? In what ways is he positive? Give evidence from the text in support of your views.

9 Write an essay on 'sick' or 'black' humour in the novel, saying what effect it has on one's appreciation of the book.

10 What reasons are there for asserting that the intention behind *Catch-22* is a serious one? Give reasons for your answer.

11 Write an appreciation of the presentation of eccentricity in *Catch-22* with reference to at least *three* or *four* men.

12 'Men without women.' How far does this define the situation on Pianosa?

13 In what ways does the humour reflect the need to escape from the *Catch-22* situation?

14 Write an essay on Heller's use of imagery in *Catch-22*.

15 Examine Heller's use of symbol.

16 Which of Heller's stylistic effects do you find most interesting in this book, and why?

17 In what ways is *Catch-22* different from any other novel you have read?

18 'It is an all-out attack on the establishment.' Discuss this view of *Catch-22*.

19 Write a detailed appreciation of the structure of the book.

20 In what ways has *Catch-22* 'dated'? Give reasons for your answer.

21 'Obsessed with sex and the grotesque'. How far would you agree with this judgement of *Catch-22*?

Further reading

John Wain: *Catch-22* (*Critical Quarterly*, Summer 1963)

Anthony Burgess: *The Novel Today* (1967)

Bernard Bergonzi: *The Situation of the Novel* (1970)

Tony Tanner: *City of Words: American Fiction 1950–1970* (1971)

Jerry Bryant: *The Open Decision: The Contemporary American Novel and its Intellectual Background* (1970)

Jan Solomon *The Structure of Joseph Heller's Catch-22* in *Studies in Modern Fiction* 9(2), pp.46–57